PHILIP'S ROAD ATLAS

CON BRITAIN

II	Key to road map symbols
III	Distance table
IV	Counties map
1	**Key to map pages**
2	**Road maps of Great Britain** at 8 miles to 1 inch
58	**Road maps of Ireland** at 19 miles to 1 inch
62	Index to road maps of Ireland
64	Index to road maps of Great Britain

www.philips-maps.co.uk

First published in 2010 by Philip's
a division of Octopus Publishing Group Ltd
www.octopusbooks.co.uk
Carmelite House
50 Victoria Embankment
London EC4Y 0DZ
An Hachette UK Company
www.hachette.co.uk

Third edition 2015, first impression 2015

ISBN 978-1-84907-395-0

Cartography by Philip's, copyright © 2015 Philip's

 **Ordnance Survey®** This product includes mapping data
licensed from Ordnance Survey®,
with the permission of the Controller
of Her Majesty's Stationery Office. © Crown copyright 2015. All
rights reserved. Licence number 100011710

 The map of Ireland on pages 58–61 is based upon the
Crown Copyright and is reproduced with the
permission of Land & Property Services under
delegated authority from the Controller of Her Majesty's
Stationery Office, © Crown Copyright and database right 2015,
PMLPA No 100503, and on Ordnance Survey Ireland by
permission of the Government © Ordnance Survey Ireland /
Government of Ireland Permit number 8982.

Printed in China

*Independent research survey, from research carried out by
Outlook Research Limited, 2005/06.

**Nielsen BookScan Travel Publishing Year Book 2014 data

Road map symbols

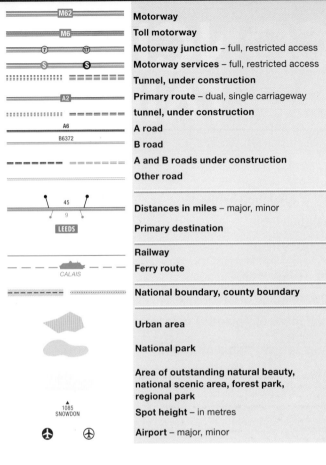

Motorway

Toll motorway

Motorway junction – full, restricted access

Motorway services – full, restricted access

Tunnel, under construction

Primary route – dual, single carriageway

tunnel, under construction

A road

B road

A and B roads under construction

Other road

Distances in miles – major, minor

Primary destination

Railway

Ferry route

National boundary, county boundary

Urban area

National park

Area of outstanding natural beauty, national scenic area, forest park, regional park

Spot height – in metres

Airport – major, minor

Abbreviated local authority areas

BD	Bridgend	13 G12
BF	Bracknell Forest	16 J3
BG	Blaenau Gwent	13 E15
BL	Blackpool	26 B4
BM	Bournemouth	8 H5
BN	Blackburn with Darwen	27 C8
CB	City and County of Bristol	14 J4
CBH	City of Brighton and Hove	10 J3
CE	City of Edinburgh	40 F5
CF	Cardiff	7 C10
CM	Clackmannanshire	40 D2
CN	City of Nottingham	22 A4
CY	Caerphilly	7 B10
DD	Dundee City	51 P3
DE	Derby City	22 B2
DN	Darlington	32 C4
ED	East Dunbartonshire	39 C11
ER	East Renfrewshire	39 E9
FK	Falkirk	39 C13
GC	Glasgow City	39 D10
HL	Hartlepool	32 A6
HN	Halton	26 G6
IC	Inverclyde	39 D8
KH	Kingston upon Hull	29 A9
LE	Leicester City	22 E5
LU	Luton	16 C5
MB	Middlesbrough	32 C6
MR	Merthyr Tydfil	13 E14
NEL	North East Lincolnshire	29 D11
NL	North Lanarkshire	39 D13
NP	Newport	7 C12
NPT	Neath Port Talbot	13 F11
PL	Plymouth	3 F12
PM	Portsmouth	9 G11
PO	Poole	8 H5
RC	Redcar and Cleveland	33 C8
RD	Reading	16 H2
RF	Renfrewshire	39 D9
RT	Rhondda Cynon Taff	7 B9
SD	Southend-on-Sea	17 G14
SL	Slough	16 G4
SN	Stockton-on-Tees	32 B6
SO	Southampton	9 F9
ST	Stoke-on-Trent	21 A9
SW	Swindon	15 G10
TB	Torbay	4 G2
TF	Torfaen	7 A11
TK	Thurrock	17 G12
TW	Telford and Wrekin	20 E7
WA	Warrington	26 G7
WD	West Dunbartonshire	39 C9
WK	Wokingham	16 J2
WL	West Lothian	40 F3
WM	Windsor and Maidenhead	16 H3

Scales

Pages 2–56

1:506 880, 1cm = 5.07 km, 1 in = 8 miles

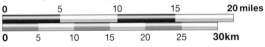

```
0        5        10       15       20 miles
0     5    10    15    20    25    30km
```

Pages 58–61

1:1 200 000, 1cm = 12km, 1 in = 18.94 miles

```
0       10       20      30 miles
0    10    20    30    40    50km
```

Distance table

How to use this table

Distances are shown in miles and, in light type, kilometres. For example, the distance between Birmingham and Dover is **194** miles or 312 kilometres.

London
517 / 832 **Aberdeen**
211 445 / 340 716 **Aberystwyth**
117 420 114 / 188 676 183 **Birmingham**
107 564 207 147 / 172 908 333 237 **Bournemouth**
52 573 253 163 92 / 84 922 407 262 148 **Brighton**
122 493 125 81 82 147 / 196 793 201 130 132 237 **Bristol**
54 471 214 100 154 116 169 / 87 758 344 161 248 187 272 **Cambridge**
157 505 105 103 117 182 45 190 / 253 813 169 166 188 293 72 306 **Cardiff**
301 221 224 196 343 370 277 264 465 / 484 356 360 315 552 596 446 425 465 **Carlisle**
71 588 297 194 174 82 202 125 238 389 / 114 947 478 312 280 132 325 201 383 626 **Dover**
448 67 376 349 495 517 430 406 441 152 523 / 721 108 605 562 797 832 692 654 710 245 842 **Dundee**
390 125 320 292 439 456 373 345 385 96 462 56 / 628 201 515 470 707 734 600 555 620 154 744 90 **Edinburgh**
260 504 56 170 222 291 154 270 112 297 331 460 399 / 418 811 90 274 357 468 248 435 180 478 533 740 642 **Fishguard**
510 149 430 392 539 575 486 479 485 206 596 127 144 486 / 821 240 692 631 867 926 782 771 781 332 959 204 232 782 **Fort William**
397 145 320 292 439 468 373 372 385 96 488 83 44 376 101 / 639 233 515 470 707 753 600 599 620 154 786 134 71 605 163 **Glasgow**
109 468 102 56 99 159 35 123 56 247 191 410 349 153 454 346 / 175 753 164 90 159 256 56 198 90 398 307 660 562 246 731 557 **Gloucester**
76 535 281 167 187 128 217 67 246 336 125 469 413 337 543 432 196 / 122 861 452 269 301 206 349 108 396 541 201 755 665 542 874 695 316 **Harwich**
269 439 111 148 288 334 206 270 216 231 360 394 333 167 438 330 191 349 / 433 707 179 238 463 538 332 435 348 372 580 634 536 269 705 531 307 562 **Holyhead**
550 105 486 458 597 617 539 505 549 262 622 132 158 542 66 166 504 569 474 / 885 169 782 737 961 993 867 813 884 422 1001 212 254 872 106 267 811 916 763 **Inverness**
663 232 601 574 724 741 668 630 680 391 746 259 285 671 195 295 628 693 603 129 / 1067 373 967 924 1165 1193 1075 1014 1094 629 1201 417 459 1080 314 475 1011 1116 970 208 **John o' Groats**
184 364 223 134 264 245 233 139 244 158 256 295 254 169 196 231 394 518 / 296 586 359 216 425 394 375 224 393 254 412 475 377 451 594 409 272 316 372 634 834 **Kingston upon Hull**
297 692 313 281 205 308 200 374 245 477 381 642 574 353 686 573 235 390 405 741 868 421 / 478 1114 504 452 330 496 322 602 394 768 613 1033 924 568 1104 922 378 628 652 1193 1397 678 **Land's End**
189 327 169 113 255 260 194 145 232 119 260 258 202 237 329 215 176 360 487 55 405 / 304 526 272 182 410 419 312 233 373 192 418 415 325 381 530 346 280 359 283 579 784 89 652 **Leeds**
131 383 199 90 209 197 183 85 208 191 202 314 258 272 399 291 159 155 216 427 554 44 371 68 / 211 616 320 145 336 317 295 137 335 307 325 505 415 438 642 468 256 249 348 687 892 71 597 109 **Lincoln**
202 341 104 93 234 272 161 194 169 120 299 286 216 160 329 216 140 265 102 382 511 130 361 75 129 / 325 549 167 150 377 438 259 312 272 193 481 460 348 257 530 348 225 427 164 615 822 209 581 121 208 **Liverpool**
185 340 129 80 227 257 161 165 183 119 276 285 215 197 329 215 126 228 124 373 500 95 361 40 84 35 / 298 547 208 129 365 414 259 266 295 192 444 459 346 317 530 346 203 367 200 600 805 153 581 64 135 56 **Manchester**
286 235 257 207 347 352 299 241 325 57 358 166 110 329 253 146 266 308 272 268 395 132 498 92 159 168 132 / 460 378 414 333 558 567 481 388 523 92 576 267 177 529 407 238 428 496 438 431 636 212 802 148 256 270 212 **Newcastle upon Tyne**
114 496 256 174 175 252 62 262 289 174 422 366 343 504 385 204 73 311 529 654 149 421 176 105 220 185 264 / 183 798 444 267 344 282 406 100 422 465 280 679 589 552 811 620 328 117 501 852 1053 240 678 283 169 354 298 425 **Norwich**
57 483 154 64 90 108 74 83 108 260 141 433 372 205 472 356 52 145 238 532 656 152 274 168 137 172 144 260 145 / 92 777 248 103 145 174 119 134 174 418 227 697 599 330 760 573 84 233 383 856 1056 309 441 270 221 277 232 418 233 **Oxford**
218 615 237 203 128 224 122 293 167 399 300 642 496 264 595 495 157 309 368 790 805 89 316 293 283 283 410 343 199 / 351 990 382 327 206 361 196 472 269 642 483 888 798 425 958 797 253 497 528 1069 1271 571 143 509 472 455 455 660 552 320 **Plymouth**
159 360 159 76 216 226 161 120 194 152 245 291 235 215 348 248 126 187 168 393 520 65 361 33 46 72 38 125 146 135 283 / 256 579 256 122 348 364 259 193 312 245 394 468 378 346 560 399 203 301 270 632 837 105 581 53 74 116 61 201 235 217 455 **Sheffield**
77 547 201 128 31 61 76 148 121 324 143 500 438 233 541 433 105 164 293 598 723 256 232 204 239 221 324 206 64 151 199 / 124 880 323 206 50 98 122 238 195 521 230 805 705 375 871 697 169 264 472 963 1164 412 367 373 328 385 356 521 332 103 243 320 **Southampton**
402 228 325 297 444 475 378 379 390 101 496 167 124 392 195 84 343 410 338 262 379 259 585 220 298 221 220 158 403 379 500 263 445 / 647 367 523 478 715 765 608 610 628 163 798 269 200 631 314 135 552 660 544 422 610 417 941 354 480 356 354 254 649 610 805 423 716 **Stranraer**
194 507 73 119 167 222 85 227 41 309 274 473 412 167 496 409 89 267 184 572 696 264 285 248 233 195 187 347 301 141 206 217 194 / 312 816 117 192 269 357 137 365 66 497 441 761 663 108 798 658 143 430 296 921 1120 425 459 399 375 314 301 559 485 227 332 349 259 671 **Swansea**
207 319 195 130 269 275 222 165 244 121 282 350 194 261 330 217 128 228 204 352 479 37 411 24 75 99 64 84 181 181 333 52 258 222 272 / 333 513 314 209 433 443 357 266 393 195 454 402 312 420 531 349 304 367 328 566 771 60 661 39 121 159 103 135 291 536 84 415 357 438 **York**

Map of Great Britain with cities marked: John o' Groats, Inverness, Aberdeen, Fort William, Dundee, Glasgow, Edinburgh, Stranraer, Newcastle upon Tyne, Carlisle, York, Leeds, Kingston upon Hull, Manchester, Lincoln, Holyhead, Liverpool, Sheffield, Norwich, Birmingham, Aberystwyth, Cambridge, Gloucester, Oxford, Harwich, Fishguard, Swansea, Cardiff, Bristol, London, Dover, Southampton, Brighton, Bournemouth, Plymouth, Land's End.

Counties and unitary authorities

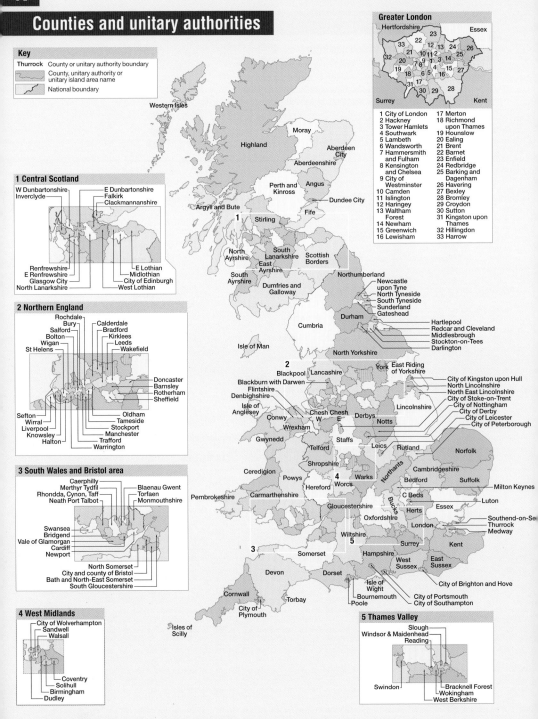

Greater London

Hertfordshire
Essex
Surrey
Kent

1 City of London
2 Hackney
3 Tower Hamlets
4 Southwark
5 Lambeth
6 Wandsworth
7 Hammersmith and Fulham
8 Kensington and Chelsea
9 City of Westminster
10 Camden
11 Islington
12 Haringey
13 Waltham Forest
14 Newham
15 Greenwich
16 Lewisham
17 Merton
18 Richmond upon Thames
19 Hounslow
20 Ealing
21 Brent
22 Barnet
23 Enfield
24 Redbridge
25 Barking and Dagenham
26 Havering
27 Bexley
28 Bromley
29 Croydon
30 Sutton
31 Kingston upon Thames
32 Hillingdon
33 Harrow

Key

Thurrock — County or unitary authority boundary
County, unitary authority or unitary island area name
National boundary

Western Isles

1 Central Scotland

W Dunbartonshire
Inverclyde
E Dunbartonshire
Falkirk
Clackmannanshire

Renfrewshire
E Renfrewshire
Glasgow City
North Lanarkshire
E Lothian
Midlothian
City of Edinburgh
West Lothian

2 Northern England

Rochdale
Bury
Salford
Bolton
Wigan
St Helens
Calderdale
Bradford
Kirklees
Leeds
Wakefield

Doncaster
Barnsley
Rotherham
Sheffield

Sefton
Wirral
Liverpool
Knowsley
Halton
Oldham
Tameside
Stockport
Manchester
Trafford
Warrington

3 South Wales and Bristol area

Caerphilly
Merthyr Tydfil
Rhondda, Cynon, Taff
Neath Port Talbot
Blaenau Gwent
Torfaen
Monmouthshire

Swansea
Bridgend
Vale of Glamorgan
Cardiff
Newport

North Somerset
City and county of Bristol
Bath and North-East Somerset
South Gloucestershire

4 West Midlands

City of Wolverhampton
Sandwell
Walsall

Coventry
Solihull
Birmingham
Dudley

5 Thames Valley

Slough
Windsor & Maidenhead
Reading

Swindon
Bracknell Forest
Wokingham
West Berkshire

Highland
Moray
Aberdeen City
Aberdeenshire
Perth and Kinross
Angus
Argyll and Bute
Dundee City
Stirling
Fife
North Ayrshire
South Lanarkshire
East Ayrshire
Scottish Borders
South Ayrshire
Dumfries and Galloway
Northumberland
Newcastle upon Tyne
North Tyneside
South Tyneside
Sunderland
Gateshead
Durham
Hartlepool
Redcar and Cleveland
Middlesbrough
Stockton-on-Tees
Darlington
Cumbria
Isle of Man
North Yorkshire
Blackpool
Lancashire
York
East Riding of Yorkshire
Blackburn with Darwen
Flintshire
Denbighshire
Isle of Anglesey
Conwy
Chesh W
Chesh E
Derbys
Notts
Wrexham
Gwynedd
Staffs
Telford
Leics
Rutland
Norfolk
Shropshire
Ceredigion
Warks
Northants
Cambridgeshire
Powys
Hereford
Worcs
Bedford
Suffolk
Pembrokeshire
Carmarthenshire
C Beds
Milton Keynes
Gloucestershire
Bucks
Essex
Luton
Oxfordshire
Herts
Southend-on-Sea
London
Thurrock
Medway
Wiltshire
Surrey
Kent
Somerset
Hampshire
West Sussex
East Sussex
Devon
Dorset
Isle of Wight
City of Brighton and Hove
Cornwall
Torbay
Bournemouth
Poole
City of Portsmouth
City of Southampton
City of Plymouth
Isles of Scilly
City of Kingston upon Hull
North Lincolnshire
North East Lincolnshire
City of Stoke-on-Trent
City of Nottingham
City of Derby
City of Leicester
City of Peterborough
Lincolnshire

Key to map pages

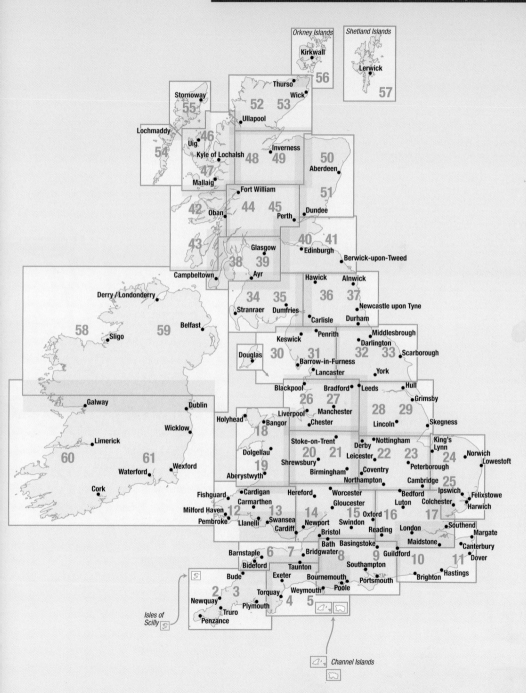

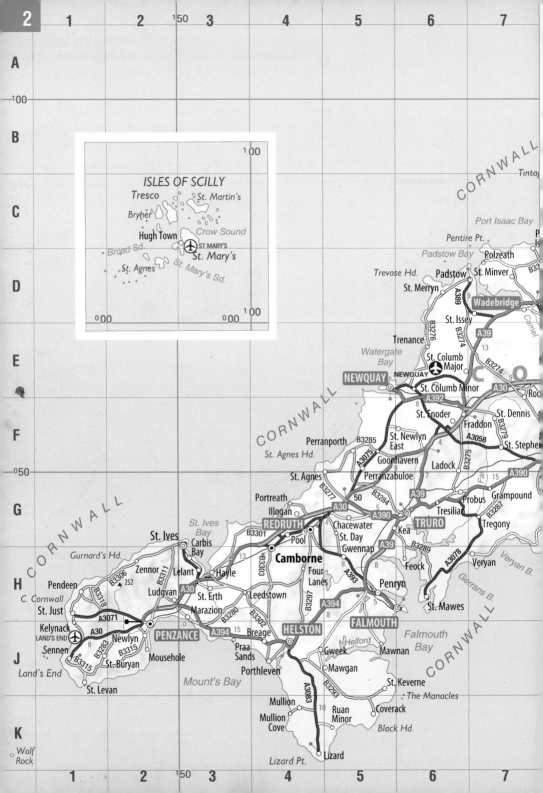

2

1 150 3 4 5 6 7

100

ISLES OF SCILLY

Tresco
St. Martin's
Bryher
Crow Sound
Hugh Town
Broad Sd.
ST MARY'S
St. Mary's
St. Agnes
St. Mary's Sd.

100

0 00 0 00

CORNWALL

Tintag

Port Isaac Bay

Pentire Pt.
P
Is
Polzeath
B33
Trevose Hd.
St. Minver
Padstow
Padstow Bay
St. Merryn
A389
Wadebridge
St. Issey
B3276
B3274
13
A39
Trenance
B3274
Watergate
Bay
St. Columb
Major
Camel
NEWQUAY
NEWQUAY
St. Columb Minor
A30
Ro
C   O
8
A392
St. Enoder
St. Dennis
Fraddon
B3279
Perranporth
B3285
St. Newlyn
East
Ladock
A3058
St. Stepher
St. Agnes Hd.
Goonhavern
4
B3275
Fal
St. Agnes
Perranzabuloe
A39
B3284
B3277
50
Probus
Grampound
Portreath
A30
A390
Tresilian
B3287
Tregony
Illogan
A390
Kea
Ladock
15
A390
REDRUTH
Chacewater
TRURO
St. Ives
Bay
B3301
Pool
St. Day
B3289
Veryan
Carbis
Bay
Gwennap
A3078
Veryan B.
St. Ives
13
Camborne
Feock
Gurnard's Hd.
B3303
Four
Lanes
A393
St. Mawes
Zennor
B3311
Lelant
Hayle
Penryn
Gerrans B.
Pendeen
252
Ludgvan
St. Erth
Leedstown
B3297
PENRYN
CORNWALL
C. Cornwall
B3306
A30
A394
FALMOUTH
St. Just
B3318
Marazion
B3280
B3302
A394
Breage
HELSTON
Falmouth
Bay
Kelynack
A3071
15
Gweek
LAND'S END
A30
PENZANCE
Praa
Sands
Helford
Mawnan
Newlyn
B3293
Sennen
B3315
Mousehole
Porthleven
Mawgan
St. Keverne
St. Buryan
Mount's Bay
B3293
The Manacles
St. Levan
A3083
Mullion
Ruan
Minor
Coverack
Wolf
Rock
Mullion
Cove
10
Black Hd.
Lizard Pt.
Lizard

1 150 3 4 5 6 7

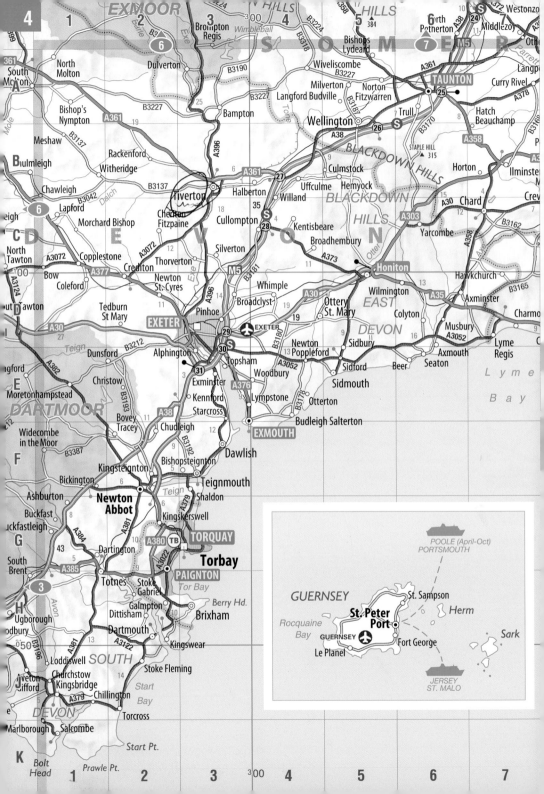

WARWICKSHIRE

STRATFORD-UPON-AVON

Feckenham · Studley · Astwood Bank · Alcester · Wootton Wawen · Barford · Harbury · Southam · Stockton · Daventry · Weedon Bec

Inkberrow · Bidford-on-Avon · Wellesbourne · Gaydon · Fenny Compton · Byfield · Arbury Hill 224

Upton Snodsbury · Salford Priors · Cleeve Prior · Kineton · Ettington · **BANBURY** · Wardington · Middleton Cheney

EVESHAM · Harvington · Bretforton · Mickleton · Halford · Shipston-on-Stour · Wroxton · King's Sutton · Brackley · Aynho

Eckington · Ashton under Hill · Broadway · Chipping Campden · Blockley · Moreton-in-Marsh · Long Compton · Hook Norton · Bloxham · Deddington · Ardley · Bicester

Bredon Hill · Stanway · Bishop's Cleeve · Winchcombe · Swalcliffe · Charlbury · Middle Barton · Upper Heyford · Ambrosden

Prestbury · Stow-on-the-Wold · Churchill · Enstone · Kirtlington · Bletchingdon · Islip

CHELTENHAM · Charlton Kings · Andoversford · Bourton-on-the-Water · Chipping Norton · Woodstock · Kidlington · Stanton St. John

Withington · Northleach · Shipton under Wychwood · Witney · Yarnton · **OXFORD** · Wheatley

COTSWOLDS · Burford · Aldsworth · Brize Norton · Carterton · Stanton Harcourt · Eynsham · Botley · Kennington

North Cerney · Bibury · Bampton · Standlake · Cumnor · Sandleigh · Radley

CIRENCESTER · Fairford · Lechlade-on-Thames · Buckland · Kingston Bagpuize · **Abingdon-on-Thames**

South Cerney · Kemble · Ashton Keynes · Cricklade · Highworth · Faringdon · Grove · Dorchester · Sutton Courtenay · Benson

Minety · Charlton · Purton · Stratton St. Margaret · Watchfield · Shrivenham · Uffington · Wantage · Harwell · **Didcot** · Blewbury · Cholsey

Brinkworth · **SWINDON** · Wanborough · Ashbury · White Horse Hill · Lambourn · Farnborough · East Ilsley · Streatley · Compton · Pangbourne

Great Somerford · Royal Wootton Bassett · Wroughton · Chiseldon · Aldbourne · Great Shefford · Hampstead Norreys

CHIPPENHAM · Calne · Broad Hinton · Ogbourne St. George · Whitonditch · Welford · Hermitage · Theale

Melksham · Lacock · Cherhill · Avebury · **MARLBOROUGH** · Hungerford · **NEWBURY** · Thatcham

Bromham · Beckhampton · Froxfield · Walbury Hill 297 · East Woodhay · Burghclere

Devizes · Pewsey · Burbage

BERKSHIRE DOWNS · NORTH WESSEX · WEST BERKSHIRE · MARLBOROUGH DOWNS · Vale of White Horse

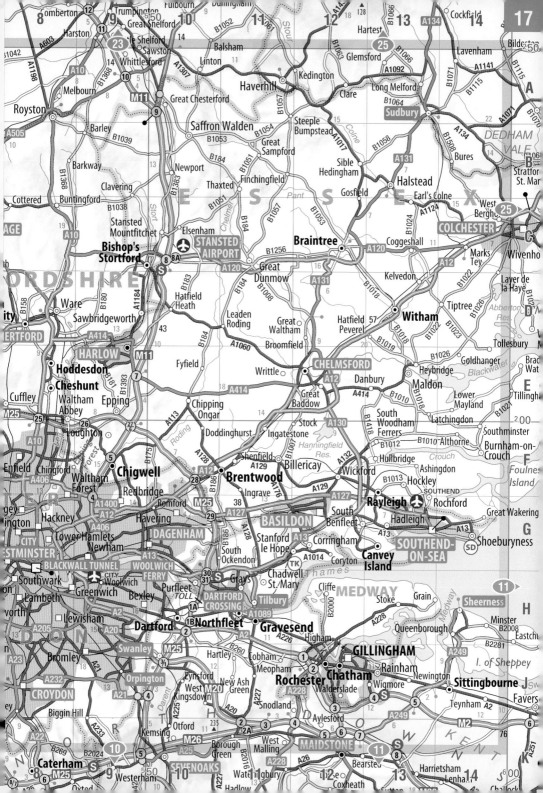

YORKSHIRE

8 9 10 11 12 13 14

A B C D E F G H J K

Leven
Skirlaugh
Aldbrough
Beverley
33
North Newbald
Cottingham
KH
Sproatley
Marfleet
Preston
KINGSTON UPON HULL
Hedon
Withernsea
Hessle
Paull
Burstwick
Hollym
HUMBER BRIDGE
South Cave
North Ferriby
New Holland
Keyingham
Patrington
Easington
Barton upon Humber
Barrow upon Humber
Sunk Island
Kilnsea
Winterton
Bonby
Ulceby
A160
Immingham
Stallingborough
Spurn Hd.
SCUNTHORPE
Broughton
Keelby
A180
GRIMSBY
Cleethorpes
ZEEBRUGGE ROTTERDAM
Brigg
Barnetby le Wold
Laceby
Waltham
Humberston
Mouth of the Humber
Hibaldstow
Grasby
HUMBERSIDE
New Waltham
NEL
Tetney
Marshchapel
Donna Nook
South Kelsey
Caistor
Nettleton
Grainthorpe
North Somercotes
Waddingham
Normanby le Wold
North Thoresby
Ludborough
Saltfleet
Caenby Corner
Usselby
Binbrook
Saltfleetby
West Rasen
Faldingworth
Market Rasen
Ludford
South Elkington
Louth
Manby
Mablethorpe
Hainton
Legbourne
Sutton-on-Sea
LINCOLNSHIRE WOLDS
Scamblesby
Withern
Maltby le Marsh
Huttoft
Stainton
Wragby
Belchford
Alford
Chapel St. Leonards
Nettleham
Ulceby Cross
Willoughby
Washingborough
Bardney
Horncastle
Hagworthingham
Partney
Ingoldmells
LINCOLN
Branston
Spilsby
Burgh le Marsh
Bracebridge Heath
Old Bolingbroke
SKEGNESS
North Hykeham
Metheringham
Woodhall Spa
Mareham le Fen
Wainfleet All Saints
Waddington
Scopwick
Coningsby
Stickney
Stickford
Gibraltar Pt.
Navenby
Digby
Walcott
Billinghay
West Fen
East Fen
Welbourn
Cranwell
Ruskington
Sibsey
Wrangle
Leasingham
Brothertoft
Old Leake
Sleaford
23
Ancaster
Heckingt
Holland Fen
BOSTON
23
Fishtoft

8   9   10   11   5 00   12   13   14

A

B

REDCAR
Marske-by-the-Sea
Saltburn-by-the-Sea
A174
Skelton
Brotton
Loftus   Staithes
A173   RC   23   A174   Kettle Ness
Guisborough   B1366   Hinderwell
A171   20   Lythe
yton   51   WHITBY
Castleton   Egton   Sneaton
Esk   Hawsker
Sleights
ND HILLS   Goathland   Robin Hood's Bay
▲454   Fylingdales
RTH YORK MOORS   Moor   19   Staintondale
NATIONAL PARK   A169   5 00
Rosedale   A171
Abbey   Cloughton
Hodge   20   Burniston
Hutton-le-Hole   Lockton   Scalby
Dove   Seven   Ayton   SCARBOROUGH
Kirkbymoorside   A165
evaulx   27   A170   Thornton-le-   Eastfield
Helmsley   Dale   16   Ebberston   B1261
Pickering   A170   Seamer
Vale of Pickering   Snainton   A64   Filey
Rye   B1258   Sherburn-   Staxton   17
Hovingham   The Carrs   Hunmanby
HOWARDIAN   B1257   21   B1249   Burton   Filey Bay
HILLS   Malton   Rillington   Fleming   B1229
Terrington   A64   Weaverthorpe   A165   Flamborough
Norton   B1253   B1255   Flamborough
llington   Sheriff   Rudston   Hd.
Hutton   B1248   Langtoft   BRIDLINGTON
Acklam   B1253   Kilham   A614   Burton
Strensall   Fridaythorpe   Sledmere   13   Agnes   Bridlington
19   Garton-on-   Nafferton
Haxby   A64   the-Wolds   Lissett   Bay
New Earswick   A166   Wetwang   Driffield
Stamford   30   B1249   Beeford   Skipsea
YORK   Bridge   Bainton   North   46
Dunnington   Hutton   Frodingham   B1242
CITY   A1079   Cranswick   Hornsea
OF   A1079   19   B1246   A164   A165   4 50
YORK   Elvington   Barmby   Pocklington   Leven   B1244
A19   Moor   A614   Middleton on   B1240
Wheldrake   Hayton   the Wolds
Escrick   Market   YORKSHIRE   A1035   laugh
all   16   Weighton   B1248   Aldbrough
8   9   10   11   5 00   12   13   14

C

D

E

F

G

H

J

K

EAST RIDING
OF
YORKSHIRE

28   29

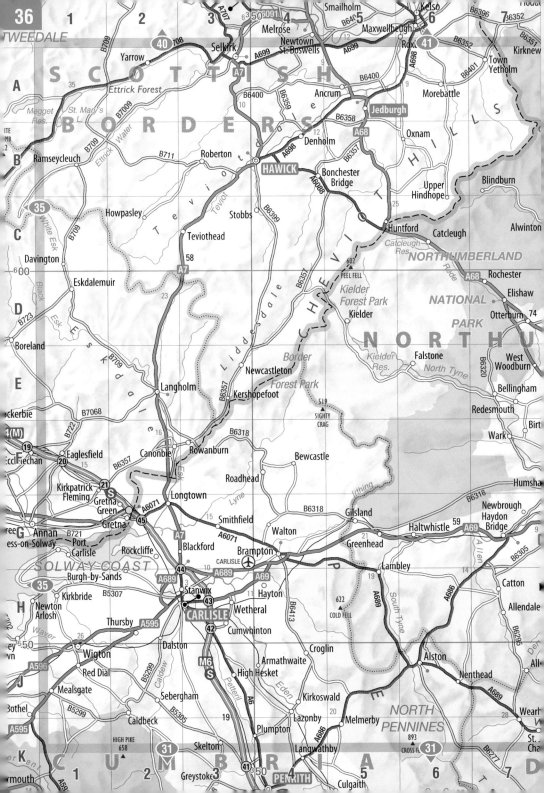

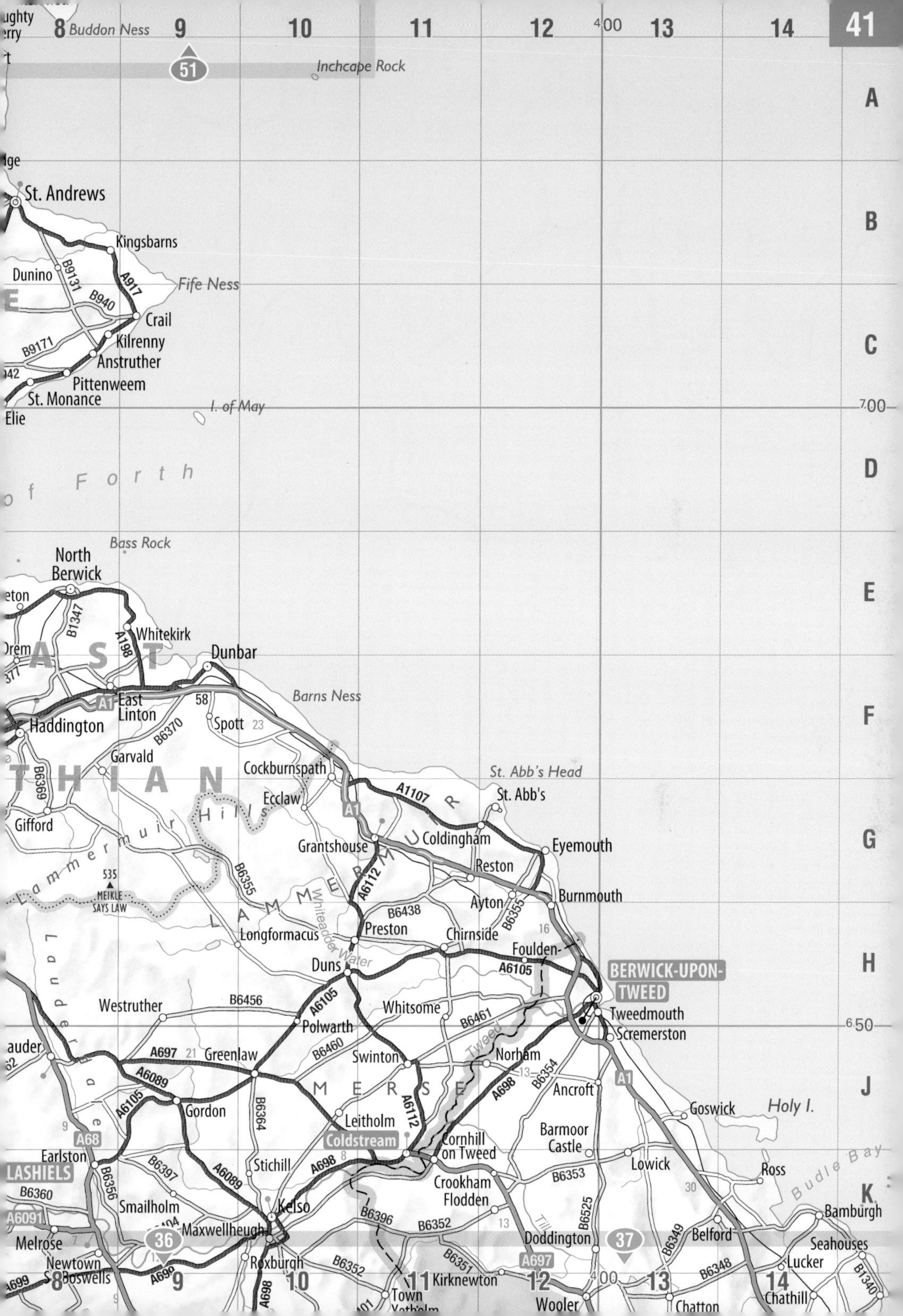

Buddon Ness
Inchcape Rock
51
St. Andrews
Kingsbarns
Dunino
B9131
A917
B940
Fife Ness
Crail
Kilrenny
B9171
Anstruther
Pittenweem
St. Monance
Elie
I. of May
o f F o r t h
Bass Rock
North Berwick
B1347
A198
Whitekirk
Dunbar
East Linton
A1
Haddington
B6370
58
Spott
23
Barns Ness
Garvald
B6369
Cockburnspath
Gifford
Ecclaw
A1107
St. Abb's Head
St. Abb's
Lammermuir Hills
Grantshouse
Coldingham
Eyemouth
535
MEIKLE SAYS LAW
B6355
A6112
Reston
LAMMERMUIR
Ayton
Burnmouth
B6438
Whiteadder Water
Preston
Longformacus
Chirnside
16
Foulden
Duns
A6105
BERWICK-UPON-TWEED
Westruther
B6456
Whitsome
Tweedmouth
Polwarth
B6461
Scremerston
Lauder
A697
21
Greenlaw
B6460
Swinton
Tweed
Norham
13
A6089
B6354
Ancroft
A698
MERSE
Gordon
B6364
A6112
Leitholm
Goswick
Holy I.
A68
Earlston
Coldstream
Barmoor Castle
Cornhill on Tweed
Budle Bay
LASHIELS
B6397
Stichill
A698
B6353
Lowick
Ross
B6360
B6356
A6089
Crookham
Flodden
30
Smailholm
Kelso
B6525
Bamburgh
A6091
Maxwellheugh
B6396
B6352
13
Till
B6349
Belford
Melrose
36
37
Doddington
Seahouses
Newtown St. Boswells
Roxburgh
B6352
B6351
A697
B6348
Lucker
A699
Kirknewton
B1340
A698
Town Yetholm
Wooler
Chatton
Chathill
8
9
10
11
12
13
14
400
700
650
A
B
C
D
E
F
G
H
J
K

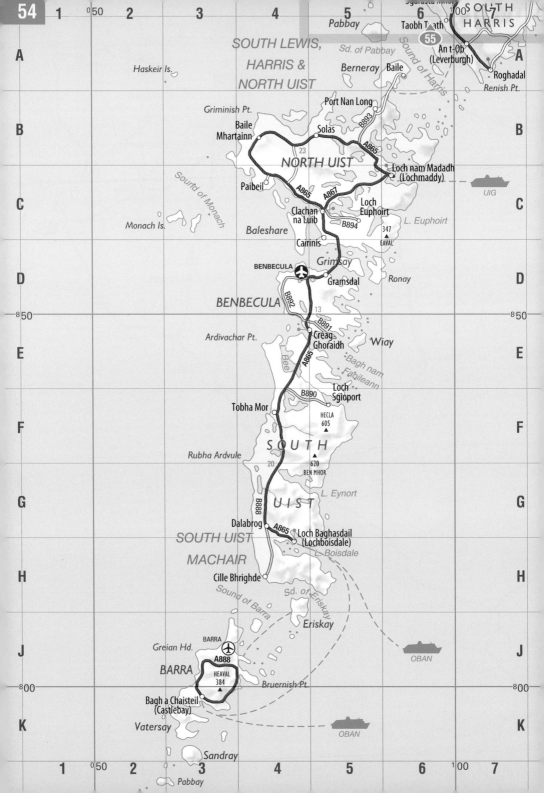

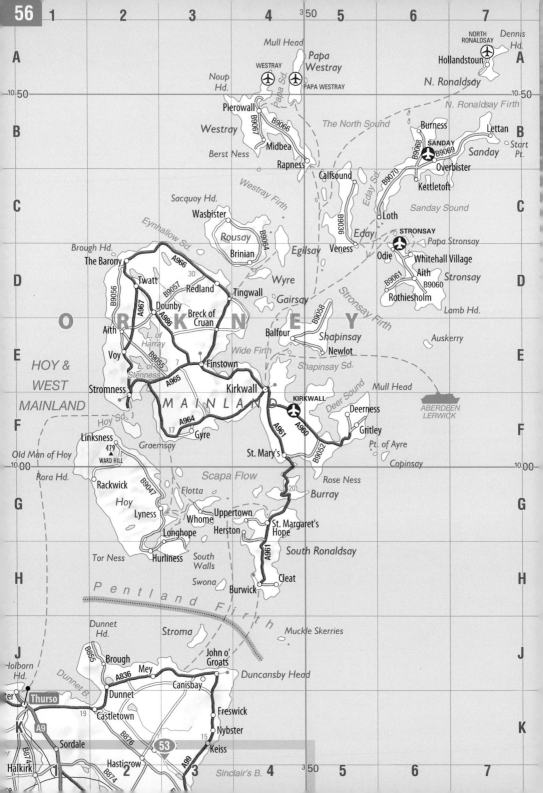

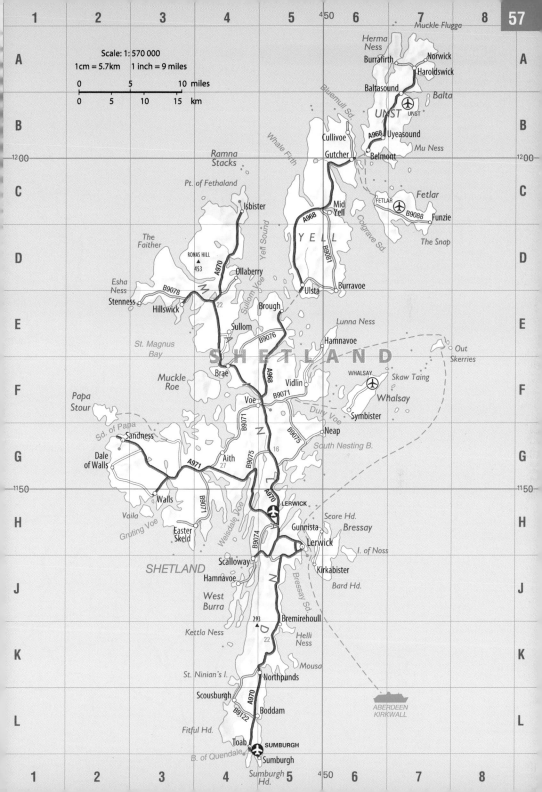

Scale: 1: 570 000
1cm = 5.7km   1 inch = 9 miles

0   5   10 miles
0   5   10   15   km

Muckle Flugga

Herma
Ness

Burrafirth   Norwick
                          Haroldswick
        Baltasound

Bluemull Sd.   Balta

        UNST   UNST
Whale Firth

Cullivoe   Uyeasound
A968

Gutcher   Belmont   Mu Ness

Ramna
Stacks

1200   1200

Pt. of Fethaland

Isbister   Mid   FETLAR   Fetlar
                Yell   B9088   Funzie

The
Faither   A968   YELL   Cograve Sd.

RONAS HILL   The Snap
▲
453   Ollaberry   B9081

A970   Ulsta   Burravoe

Esha   B9078
Ness   Lunna Ness
Stenness   Brough
Hillswick   22   Sullom   Hamnavoe   Out
                B9076   Skerries

                Sullom Voe

St. Magnus   SHETLAND
Bay

Muckle   Brae   A968   WHALSAY   Skaw Taing
Roe   Vidlin   WHALSAY
                        B9071   Whalsay

Papa   Voe   B9071
Stour   Symbister
        Sd. of Papa   Duru Voe
                B9075
Sandness   A971   Neap

Dale   Aith   16   South Nesting B.
of Walls   27
                B9075
1150   1150

        B9071   A970
Walls   LERWICK

Vaila   Gunnista   Score Hd.   Bressay
                                        I. of Noss
Easter   B9074   Lerwick
Skeld   Gruting Voe   Kirkabister

SHETLAND   Scalloway   Bard Hd.

        Hamnavoe   Weisdale Voe   Bressay Sd.

West   293
Burra   ▲
        22   Bremirehoull

Kettla Ness   A970   Helli
                                Ness

                Mousa   ABERDEEN
St. Ninian's I.   KIRKWALL

        Northpunds

Scousburgh   A970
        Boddam
B9122

Fitful Hd.

        Toab   SUMBURGH
B. of Quendale   Sumburgh

Sumburgh
Hd.

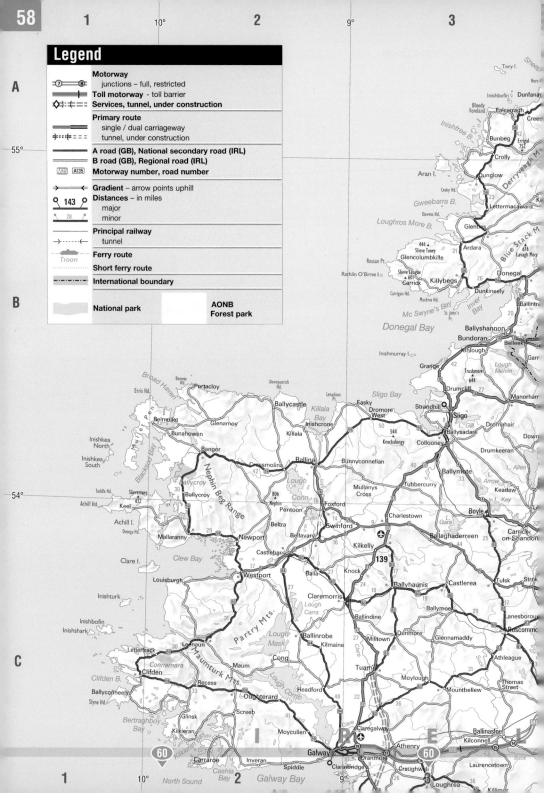

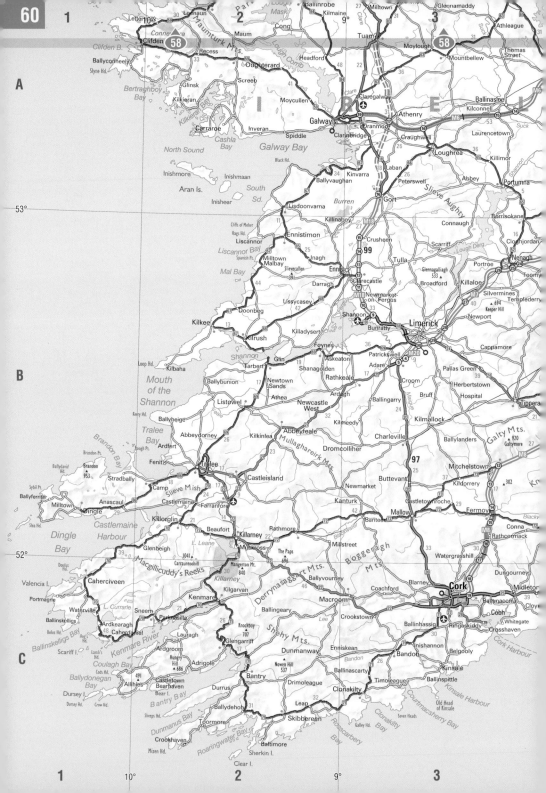

A

Abbey 60 A3
Abbeydorney. 60 B2
Abbeyfeale. 60 B2
Abbeyleix 61 B4
Adare 60 B3
Adrigole 60 C2
Aghalee 59 B5
Ahoghill 59 B5
Allihies 60 C1
Anascaul 60 B1
Annalong 59 B6
Annestown. 61 B4
Antrim 59 B5
Ardagh 60 B2
Ardara. 58 B3
Ardee 59 C5
Ardfert 60 B2
Ardglass 59 B6
Ardgroom. 60 C2
Ardkearagh 60 C1
Arklow 61 B5
Armagh. 59 B5
Armoy 59 A5
Arthurstown 61 B5
Ashbourne. 59 C5
Askeaton 60 B3
Athboy 59 C5
Athea 60 B2
Athenry. 60 A3
Athleague 58 C3
Athlone. 61 A4
Athy 61 B5
Augher 59 B4
Aughnacloy 59 B5
Aughrim. 61 B5

B

Bailieborough. 59 C5
Balbriggan. 59 C5
Balla 58 C2
Ballaghaderreen 58 C3
Ballina. 58 B2
Ballinalack. 59 C4
Ballinamore. 59 B4
Ballinascarty 60 C3
Ballinasloe. 60 A3
Ballindine 58 C3
Ballingarry
    Limerick 60 B3
    Tipperary 61 B4
Ballingeary 60 C2
Ballinhassig. 60 C3
Ballinrobe. 58 C2
Ballinskelligs 60 C1
Ballinspittle. 60 C3
Ballintra. 58 B3
Ballivor. 59 C5
Ballon 61 B5
Ballybay 59 B5
Ballybofey 59 B4
Ballybunion 60 B2
Ballycanew 61 B5
Ballycarry. 59 B6
Ballycastle
    Antrim 59 A5
    Mayo 58 B2
Ballyclare 59 B6
Ballyconneely. 58 C1

Ballycotton 60 C3
Ballycroy 58 B2
Ballydehob 60 C2
Ballyferriter. 60 B1
Ballygawley 59 B4
Ballygowan 59 B6
Ballyhaunis 58 C3
Ballyheige 60 B2
Ballyjamesduff 59 C4
Ballylanders 60 B3
Ballylynan 61 B4
Ballymahon 59 C4
Ballymena 59 B5
Ballymoe 58 C3
Ballymoney 59 A5
Ballymore. 59 C4
Ballymote. 58 B3
Ballynacorra 60 C3
Ballynagore 61 A4
Ballynahinch 59 B6
Ballynure 59 B6
Ballyragget 61 B4
Ballysadare 58 B3
Ballyshannon 58 B3
Ballyvaughan 60 A2
Ballyvourney 60 C2
Ballywalter 59 B6
Baltimore. 60 C2
Baltinglass 61 B5
Banbridge 59 B5
Bandon 60 C3
Bangor
    Down 59 B6
    Mayo 58 B2
Banteer. 60 B3
Bantry 60 C2
Beaufort. 60 B2
Belcoo. 59 B4
Belfast 59 B6
Belgooly. 60 C3
Bellananagh 59 C4
Bellavary 58 C2
Belleek 58 B3
Belmullet 58 B2
Beltra 58 C2
Belturbet 59 B4
Beragh 59 B4
Birr 61 A4
Blackwater 61 B5
Blarney 60 C3
Blessington 61 A5
Borris 61 B5
Borris-in-Ossory 61 B4
Borrisokane. 60 B3
Borrisoleigh 61 B4
Boyle 58 C3
Bracklin 59 C5
Bray 61 A5
Broadford. 60 B3
Broughshane. 59 B5
Bruff 60 B3
Bunahowen 58 B2
Bunbeg. 58 A3
Bunclody 61 B5
Buncrana 59 A4
Bundoran. 58 B3
Bunmahon. 61 B4
Bunnyconnellan. 58 B2
Bunratty. 60 B3
Bushmills 59 A5
Butler's Bridge 59 B4
Buttevant. 60 B3

C

Caher 61 B4
Caherciveen 60 C1
Caherdaniel. 60 C1
Caledon 59 B5
Callan 61 B4
Camp. 60 B2
Cappamore 60 B3
Cappoquin 61 B4
Carlingford 59 B5
Carlow 61 B5
Carndonagh 59 A4
Carnew 61 B5
Carnlough 59 B6
Carraroe. 60 A2
Carrick 58 B3
Carrickart 59 A4
Carrickfergus 59 B6
Carrickmacross 59 C5
Carrick-on-
    Shannon 58 C3
Carrick-on-Suir. 61 B4
Carrigallen 59 C4
Carryduff 59 B6
Cashel. 61 B4
Castlebar 58 C2
Castlebellingham. . . .59 C5
Castleblaney 59 B5
Castlebridge 61 B5
Castlecomer 61 B4
Castlederg 59 B4
Castledermot 61 B5
Castleisland. 60 B2
Castlemaine 60 B2
Castlemartyr 60 C3
Castlepollard 59 C4
Castlerea 58 C3
Castletown
    Bearhaven. 60 C2
Castletownroche . . .60 B3
Castlewellan 59 B6
Cavan 59 C4
Celbridge 61 A5
Charlestown. 58 C3
Charleville 60 B3
Clarecastle 60 B3
Claregalway 60 A3
Claremorris 58 C3
Clarinbridge 60 A3
Clashmore 61 B4
Claudy. 59 B4
Clifden 58 C1
Clogh. 61 B4
Cloghan
    Donegal 59 B4
    Offaly 61 A4
Clogheen 61 B4
Clogher. 59 B4
Cloghjordan 60 B3
Clonakilty 60 C3
Clonaslee. 61 A4
Clondalkin. 61 A5
Clones. 59 B4
Clonmany. 59 A4
Clonmel 61 B4
Clonmellon 59 C4
Clonord. 59 C4
Clonroche 61 B5
Cloone 59 C4
Clough 59 B6
Cloyne. 60 C3

Coachford 60 C3
Coagh 59 B5
Coalisland 59 B5
Cóbh 60 C3
Coleraine 59 A5
Collon 59 C5
Collooney. 58 B3
Comber. 59 B6
Cong 58 C2
Conna 60 B3
Connaugh 60 B3
Cookstown. 59 B5
Coolgreany 61 B5
Cooneen. 59 B4
Cootehill 59 B4
Cork 60 C3
Craughwell 60 A3
Creeslough 59 A4
Creeve. 59 B5
Crolly. 58 A3
Crookhaven. 60 C2
Crookstown 60 C3
Croom. 60 B3
Crossakiel 59 C4
Crosshaven. 60 C3
Crossmolina 58 B2
Crumlin 59 B5
Crusheen 60 B3
Cullaville 59 B5
Cushendall. 59 A5

D

Daingean 61 A4
Dalkey. 61 A5
Darragh 60 B2
Delvin 59 C4
Derrygonnelly. 59 B4
Derrylin 59 B4
Derry/Londonderry. . .59 B4
Dervock 59 A5
Dingle 60 B1
Donaghadee 59 B6
Donegal 58 B3
Doonbeg. 60 B2
Downhill. 59 A5
Downpatrick. 59 B6
Dowra 58 B3
Draperstown 59 B5
Drimoleague. 60 C2
Drogheda. 59 C5
Dromahair 58 B3
Dromcolliher. 60 B3
Dromore
    Down 59 B5
    Tyrone 59 B4
Dromore West. 58 B3
Drumcliff 58 B3
Drumkeeran 58 B3
Drumquin. 59 B4
Drumshanbo 58 B3
Drumsna. 59 C4
Dublin. 61 A5
Duleek 59 C5
Dunboyne. 59 C5
Dundalk 59 B5
Dundrum 59 B6
Dunfanaghy. 59 A4
Dungannon 59 B5
Dungarvan. 61 B4
Dungiven 59 B5
Dunglow. 58 B3

Dungourney 60 C3
Dunkineely 58 B3
Dun Laoghaire 61 A5
Dunlavin. 61 A5
Dunleer 59 C5
Dunloy 59 A5
Dunmanway 60 C2
Dunmore 58 C3
Dunmore East. 61 B5
Dunmurry. 59 B5
Dunshaughlin 59 C5
Durrow 61 B4
Durrus. 60 C2

E

Easky. 58 B3
Edenderry 61 A4
Edgeworthstown . . .59 C4
Eglinton 59 A4
Emyvale 59 B5
Enfield 59 C5
Ennis 60 B3
Enniscorthy 61 B5
Enniskean 60 C3
Enniskillen 59 B4
Ennistimon 60 B2

F

Falcarragh. 58 A3
Farranfore 60 B2
Feeny 59 B4
Fenagh 59 B4
Fenit 60 B2
Ferbane 61 A4
Fermoy 60 B3
Ferns 61 B5
Fethard
    Tipperary 61 B4
    Wexford 61 B5
Finnea 59 C4
Fintona 59 B4
Fivemiletown 59 B4
Fontstown 61 A5
Foxford 58 C2
Foynes 60 B2
Freshford 61 B4

G

Galway 60 A2
Garrison 58 B3
Garvagh 59 B5
Gilford 59 B5
Glenamoy 58 B2
Glenarm 59 B6
Glenavy. 59 B5
Glenbeigh 60 B2
Glencolumbkille. 58 B3
Glendalough 61 A5
Glenealy 61 B5
Glengarriff 60 C2
Glennamaddy 58 C3
Glenties 58 B3
Glin 60 B2
Glinsk 60 A2
Gorey. 61 B5
Gort 60 A3
Gortin 59 B4

Gowran 61 B4
Graiguenamanagh . . . 61 B5
Granard 59 C4
Grange 58 B3
Greencastle 59 A5
Greenisland 59 B6
Greystones 61 A5

H

Hacketstown 61 B5
Headford 58 C2
Herbertstown 60 B3
Hillsborough 59 B5
Holycross 61 B4
Holywood 59 B6
Hospital 60 B3

I

Inagh 60 B2
Inishannon 60 C3
Inishcrone 58 B2
Inveran 60 A2
Irvinestown 59 B4

J

Johnstown 61 B4
Julianstown 59 C5

K

Kanturk 60 B3
Keadew 58 B3
Keady 59 B5
Keel 58 C1
Keenagh 59 C4
Kells
  Antrim 59 B5
  Meath 59 C5
Kenmare 60 C2
Kesh 59 B4
Kilbaha 60 B2
Kilbeggan 61 A4
Kilcock 59 C5
Kilconnell 60 A3
Kilcormac 61 A4
Kilcullen 61 A5
Kilcurry 59 B5
Kildare 61 A5
Kildorrery 60 B3
Kilgarvan 60 C2
Kilkee 60 B2
Kilkeel 59 B5
Kilkelly 58 C3
Kilkenny 61 B4
Kilkieran 60 A2
Kilkinlea 60 B2
Killadysert 60 B2
Killala 58 B2
Killaloe 60 B3
Killarney 60 B2
Killashandra 59 B4
Killashee 59 C4
Killeigh 61 A4
Killenaule 61 B4
Killimor 60 A3
Killinaboy 60 B2

Killinick 61 B5
Killorglin 60 B2
Killucan 59 C4
Killybegs 58 B3
Killyleagh 59 B6
Kilmacrenan 59 A4
Kilmacthomas 61 B4
Kilmaine 58 C2
Kilmallock 60 B3
Kilmeadan 61 B4
Kilmeedy 60 B3
Kilmore Quay 61 B5
Kilnaleck 59 C4
Kilrea 59 B5
Kilrush 60 B2
Kiltoom 58 C3
Kingarrow 58 B3
Kingscourt 59 C5
Kinlough 58 B3
Kinnegad 59 C4
Kinnitty 61 A4
Kinsale 60 C3
Kinvarra 60 A3
Kircubbin 59 B6
Knock 58 C3
Knocktopher 61 B4

L

Laban 60 A3
Lanesborough 59 C4
Laragh 61 A5
Larne 59 B6
Lauragh 60 C2
Laurencetown 60 A3
Leap 60 C2
Leenaun 58 C2
Leighlinbridge 61 B5
Leitrim 58 C3
Letterfrack 58 C2
Letterkenny 59 B4
Lettermacaward . . . 58 B3
Lifford 59 B4
Limavady 59 A5
Limerick 60 B3
Lisbellaw 59 B4
Lisburn 59 B5
Liscannor 60 B2
Lisdoonvarna 60 A2
Lismore 61 B4
Lisnaskea 59 B4
Lissycasey 60 B2
Listowel 60 B2
Littleton 61 B4
Longford 59 C4
Loughbrickland 59 B5
Loughrea 60 A3
Louisburgh 58 C2
Lucan 61 A5
Lurgan 59 B5

M

Macroom 60 C3
Maghera 59 B5
Magherafelt 59 B5
Magilligan 59 A5
Maguiresbridge 59 B4
Malahide 59 C5
Malin 59 A4
Mallaranny 58 C2

Mallow 60 B3
Manorhamilton 58 B3
Markethill 59 B5
Maum 58 C2
Middletown 59 B5
Midleton 60 C3
Milford 59 A4
Millstreet
  Cork 60 B2
  Waterford 61 B4
Milltown
  Galway 58 C3
  Kerry 60 B1
Milltown Malbay . . . 60 B2
Mitchelstown 60 B3
Moate 61 A4
Mohill 59 C4
Monaghan 59 B5
Monasterevin 61 A4
Moneygall 61 B4
Moneymore 59 B5
Mount Bellew 58 C3
Mountfield 59 B4
Mountmellick 61 A4
Mountrath 61 B4
Moville 59 A4
Moy 59 B5
Moycullen 60 A2
Moylough 58 C3
Muckross 60 B2
Muff 59 A4
Muine Bheag 61 B5
Mullanys Cross 58 B3
Mullinavat 61 B4
Mullingar 59 C4

N

Naas 61 A5
Naul 59 C5
Navan 59 C5
Nenagh 60 B3
Newbliss 59 B4
Newbridge 61 A5
Newcastle 59 B6
Newcastle West 60 B2
Newinn 61 B4
Newmarket 60 B3
Newmarket-on-
  Fergus 60 B3
Newport
  Mayo 58 C2
  Tipperary 60 B3
New Ross 61 B5
Newry 59 B5
Newtownabbey 59 B6
Newtownards 59 B6
Newtownbutler 59 B4
Newtown
  Cunningham 59 B4
Newtownhamilton . . 59 B5
Newtownmount-
  kennedy 61 A5
Newtown Sands . . . 60 B2
Newtownstewart . . . 59 B4
Ninemilehouse 61 B4

O

Oilgate 61 B5
Oldcastle 59 C4

Omagh 59 B4
Oranmore 60 A3
Oughterard 58 C2

P

Pallas Green 60 B3
Parknasilla 60 C2
Passage East 61 B5
Patrickswell 60 B3
Paulstown 61 B4
Peterswell 60 A3
Pettigo 59 B4
Plumbridge 59 B4
Pomeroy 59 B5
Pontoon 58 C2
Portacloy 58 B2
Portadown 59 B5
Portaferry 59 B6
Portarlington 61 A4
Portavogie 59 B6
Portglenone 59 B5
Portlaoise 61 A4
Portmagne 60 C1
Portroe 60 B3
Portrush 59 A5
Portstewart 59 A5
Portumna 60 A3
Poyntz Pass 59 B5

R

Randalstown 59 B5
Rathangan 61 A5
Rathcoole 61 A5
Rathcormack 60 B3
Rathdrum 61 B5
Rathfriland 59 B5
Rathkeale 60 B3
Rathmelton 59 A4
Rathmolyon 59 C5
Rathmore 60 B2
Rathmullan 59 A4
Rathnew 61 B5
Rathvilly 61 B5
Recess 58 C2
Ringaskiddy 60 C3
Roosky 59 C4
Roscommon 58 C3
Roscrea 61 B4
Rosslare 61 B5
Rosslare Harbour . . 61 B5
Rosslea 59 B4
Roundwood 61 A5
Rush 59 C5

S

Saintfield 59 B6
Sallins 61 A5
Scarriff 60 B3
Screeb 60 A2
Seskinore 59 B4
Shanagolden 60 B2
Shercock 59 C5
Shillelagh 61 B5
Silvermines 60 B3
Sion Mills 59 B4
Skerries 59 C5
Skibbereen 60 C2

Slane 59 C5
Sligo 58 B3
Sneem 60 C2
Spiddle 60 A2
St. Johnstown 59 B4
Strabane 59 B4
Stradbally 60 B1
Strandhill 58 B3
Strangford 59 B6
Stranorlar 59 B4
Strokestown 58 C3
Swanlinbar 59 B4
Swatragh 59 B5
Swinford 58 C3
Swords 59 C5

T

Tallaght 61 A5
Tallow 60 B3
Tarbert 60 B2
Templederry 60 B3
Templemore 61 B4
Termonfeckin 59 C5
Thomas Street 58 C3
Thomastown 61 B4
Thurles 61 B4
Timoleague 60 C3
Timolin 61 B5
Tipperary 60 B3
Tobermore 59 B5
Toomyvara 60 B3
Toormore 60 C2
Tralee 60 B2
Tramore 61 B4
Trim 59 C5
Tuam 58 C3
Tubbercory 58 B3
Tulla 60 B3
Tullamore 61 A4
Tullow 61 B5
Tulsk 58 C3
Tyrrellspass 61 A4

U

Urlingford 61 B4

V

Virginia 59 C4

W

Warrenpoint 59 B5
Waterford 61 B4
Watergrasshill 60 B3
Waterville 60 C1
Wellingtonbridge . . 61 B5
Westport 58 C2
Wexford 61 B5
Whitegate 60 C3
Whitehead 59 B6
Wicklow 61 B5

Y

Youghal 61 C4

Index to road maps of Great Britain

How to use the index

Example

Gillingham Dorset **5** A11

grid square
page number
county or unitary authority (only shown for duplicate names)

Abbreviations used in the index

Aberdeen **Aberdeen City**	Glasgow **City of Glasgow**	Poole **Poole**
Aberds **Aberdeenshire**	Glos **Gloucestershire**	Powys **Powys**
Ald **Alderney**	Gtr Man **Greater Manchester**	Ptsmth **Portsmouth**
Anglesey **Isle of Anglesey**	Guern **Guernsey**	Reading **Reading**
Angus **Angus**	Gwyn **Gwynedd**	Redcar **Redcar and Cleveland**
Argyll **Argyll and Bute**	Halton **Halton**	Renfs **Renfrewshire**
Bath **Bath and North East Somerset**	Hants **Hampshire**	Rhondda **Rhondda Cynon Taff**
Bedford **Bedford**	Hereford **Herefordshire**	Rutland **Rutland**
Bl Gwent **Blaenau Gwent**	Herts **Hertfordshire**	S Ayrs **South Ayrshire**
Blackburn **Blackburn with Darwen**	Highld **Highland**	S Glos **South Gloucestershire**
Blackpool **Blackpool**	Hrtlpl **Hartlepool**	S Lanark **South Lanarkshire**
Bmouth **Bournemouth**	Hull **Hull**	S Yorks **South Yorkshire**
Borders **Scottish Borders**	IoM **Isle of Man**	Scilly **Scilly**
Brack **Bracknell**	IoW **Isle of Wight**	Shetland **Shetland**
Bridgend **Bridgend**	Invclyd **Inverclyde**	Shrops **Shropshire**
Brighton **City of Brighton and Hove**	Jersey **Jersey**	Slough **Slough**
Bristol **City and County of Bristol**	Kent **Kent**	Som **Somerset**
Bucks **Buckinghamshire**	Lancs **Lancashire**	Soton **Southampton**
C Beds **Central Bedfordshire**	Leicester **City of Leicester**	Staffs **Staffordshire**
Caerph **Caerphilly**	Leics **Leicestershire**	Southend **Southend-on-Sea**
Cambs **Cambridgeshire**	Lincs **Lincolnshire**	Stirling **Stirling**
Cardiff **Cardiff**	London **Greater London**	Stockton **Stockton-on-Tees**
Carms **Carmarthenshire**	Luton **Luton**	Stoke **Stoke-on-Trent**
Ceredig **Ceredigion**	M Keynes **Milton Keynes**	Suff **Suffolk**
Ches E **Cheshire East**	M Tydf **Merthyr Tydfil**	Sur **Surrey**
Ches W **Cheshire West and Chester**	Mbro **Middlesbrough**	Swansea **Swansea**
Clack **Clackmannanshire**	Medway **Medway**	Swindon **Swindon**
Conwy **Conwy**	Mers **Merseyside**	T&W **Tyne and Wear**
Corn **Cornwall**	Midloth **Midlothian**	Telford **Telford and Wrekin**
Cumb **Cumbria**	Mon **Monmouthshire**	Thurrock **Thurrock**
Darl **Darlington**	Moray **Moray**	Torbay **Torbay**
Denb **Denbighshire**	N Ayrs **North Ayrshire**	Torf **Torfaen**
Derby **City of Derby**	N Lincs **North Lincolnshire**	V Glam **The Vale of Glamorgan**
Derbys **Derbyshire**	N Lanark **North Lanarkshire**	W Berks **West Berkshire**
Devon **Devon**	N Som **North Somerset**	W Dunb **West Dunbartonshire**
Dorset **Dorset**	N Yorks **North Yorkshire**	W Isles **Western Isles**
Dumfries **Dumfries and Galloway**	NE Lincs **North East Lincolnshire**	W Loth **West Lothian**
Dundee **Dundee City**	Neath **Neath Port Talbot**	W Mid **West Midlands**
Durham **Durham**	Newport **City and County of Newport**	W Sus **West Sussex**
E Ayrs **East Ayrshire**	Norf **Norfolk**	W Yorks **West Yorkshire**
E Dunb **East Dunbartonshire**	Northants **Northamptonshire**	Warks **Warwickshire**
E Loth **East Lothian**	Northumb **Northumberland**	Warr **Warrington**
E Renf **East Renfrewshire**	Nottingham **City of Nottingham**	Wilts **Wiltshire**
E Sus **East Sussex**	Notts **Nottinghamshire**	Windsor **Windsor and Maidenhead**
E Yorks **East Riding of Yorkshire**	Orkney **Orkney**	Wokingham **Wokingham**
Edin **City of Edinburgh**	Oxon **Oxfordshire**	Worcs **Worcestershire**
Essex **Essex**	Pboro **Peterborough**	Wrex **Wrexham**
Falk **Falkirk**	Pembs **Pembrokeshire**	York **City of York**
Fife **Fife**	Perth **Perth and Kinross**	
Flint **Flintshire**	Plym **Plymouth**	

A

Abbey Town 35 H12
Abbots Bromley 21 D11
Abbotsbury 5 E9
Aberaeron 19 P4
Aberarth 19 P4
Abercarn 7 B11
Aberchirder 50 B5
Abercraf 13 E12
Aberdare 13 F13
Aberdaron 18 H1
Aberdeen 50 G8
Aberdour 40 E4
Aberdulais 13 G11
Aberdyfi 19 L6
Aberfeldy 45 E10
Aberffraw 18 D3
Aberfoyle 44 J7
Abergavenny 14 E1
Abergele 18 C9
Abergwili 12 D8
Abergwyngregyn ...18 C6
Abergynolwyn 19 K6
Aberlady 40 E7
Abernethy 40 B4
Aberporth 12 A6
Abersoch 18 H3
Abersychan 7 A11
Abertillery 7 A11
Aberystwyth 19 M5
Abingdon-on-
 Thames 15 G14
Abington 35 A10
Aboyne 51 H4
Accrington 27 C8
Acha 42 C3
Achanalt 48 B3
Achaphubuil 44 B2
Acharacle 42 B8
Achavanich 53 D13
Achiemore 52 B5
Achiltibuie 52 H2
Achnacroish 42 D10
Achnasheen 48 C2
Achnashellach ...46 G10
Achosnich 42 B6
Achriabhach 44 C3
Acklam 33 H9
Acle 24 D8
Acomb 32 J7
Acton Burnell 20 F6
Addingham 32 J2
Adlington 26 D7
Adwick le Street....28 D4
Affric Lodge 48 F2
Ainsdale 26 D4
Aird 43 H9
Aird a Mhulaidh 55 F3
Aird Asaig Tairbeart /
 Tarbert 55 G3
Airdrie..........39 D12
Aird Uig 55 D2
Airor 47 L2
Airth 39 B14
Aisgill 31 E13
Aith
 Orkney 56 D6
 Orkney 56 E2
 Shetland 57 G4
Akeley 16 B2
Albrighton 21 F9
Alcester 15 A9
Aldborough 32 H6
Aldbourne 15 J11
Aldbrough 29 A11
Aldeburgh 25 K9
Alderbury 8 E6
Alderley Edge 27 H9
Aldermaston 9 A10
Aldershot 9 B13
Aldridge 21 F11
Aldsworth 15 E10
Aldwick 9 H14
Alexandria 39 B8
Alford
 Aberds 50 F4
 Lincs 29 G13

Alfreton 28 J3
Alfriston 10 J6
Alkham 11 E13
Allendale Town 36 H7
Allenheads 36 J7
Alloa 39 A13
Allonby 35 J11
Alltforgan 18 H9
Almondsbury 14 H5
Alness 48 B7
Alnmouth 37 B11
Alnwick 37 B10
Alphington 4 E3
Alrewas 21 E12
Alsager 21 A9
Alston 36 J6
Altanduino 53 F10
Altarnun 3 D10
Altass 52 H7
Althorne 17 F14
Althorpe 28 C7
Altnabreac Station .53 D12
Alt na h'Airbhe ...52 J3
Altnaharra 52 E7
Alton
 Hants 9 D12
 Staffs 21 B11
Altrincham 27 G8
Alva 39 A13
Alvechurch 21 J11
Alveley 21 H8
Alveston 14 H5
Alvie 49 H9
Alwinton 37 C8
Alyth 51 N1
Amble 37 C11
Ambleside 31 D9
Ambrosden 16 D1
Amersham 16 F4
Amesbury 8 C6
Amlwch 18 A4
Ammanford 13 E10
Ampleforth 32 G7
Ampthill 16 B5
Amulree 45 F11
Ancaster 23 A8
Ancroft 41 J12
Ancrum 36 A5
Andover 9 C8
Andoversford 15 E9
Andreas 30 E4
Angle 12 F2
Angmering 10 J1
Annan 35 G12
Annbank 34 A5
Annfield Plain 37 H10
Anstey 22 E4
Anstruther 41 C8
An t-Ob /
 Leverburgh 55 J2
Appleby-in-
 Westmorland 31 B12
Applecross 46 G7
Appledore
 Devon 6 J3
 Kent 11 G10
Arbroath 51 N5
Archiestown 49 D13
Ardarroch 46 G8
Ardbeg 43 P6
Ardcharnich 52 K3
Ardchyle 44 G7
Ardentinny 38 B6
Ardersier 49 C8
Ardessie 52 K2
Ardgay 52 J7
Ardhasig 55 G3
Ardingly 10 G4
Ardlamont Ho. 38 D4
Ardleigh 25 N5
Ardley 15 D14
Ardlui 44 H5
Ardlussa 43 K8
Ardnave 43 L4
Ardrishaig 38 B3
Ardrossan 38 F7
Ardtalla 43 N6
Ardtalnaig 45 F9
Ardtoe 42 A8

Ardvasar 47 L6
Ardwell
 Dumfries 34 J2
 Moray 50 E2
Arileod 42 C3
Arinagour 42 C4
Arisaig 47 N6
Armadale
 Highland 47 L6
 W Loth 40 G2
Armathwaite 36 J4
Armitage 21 E11
Armthorpe 28 D5
Arncliffe 32 G1
Arncott 16 D1
Arnisdale 47 K8
Arnold 22 A4
Arnside 31 G10
Arreton 9 J10
Arrochar 44 J5
Arundel 10 J1
Ascot 16 J4
Asfordby 22 C6
Ash
 Kent 11 D13
 Sur 9 C13
Ashbourne 21 B12
Ashburton 4 G1
Ashbury 15 H11
Ashby de-la-Zouch .22 D2
Ashchurch 15 C8
Ashford
 Derbys 27 J12
 Kent 11 E11
Ashingdon 17 F13
Ashington 37 E11
Ashley 21 C8
Ashton 26 J5
Ashton-in-
 Makerfield 26 F6
Ashton Keynes 15 G9
Ashton under Hill. .15 C9
Ashton under Lyne .27 F10
Ashurst 9 G8
Ashwater 3 B11
Ashwell 16 B7
Ashwick 8 C1
Askam-in-Furness .31 G8
Askern 28 C4
Askrigg 32 E1
Aspatria 35 J12
Astwood Bank 21 K11
Atherstone 22 F2
Atherton 26 E7
Attleborough 24 F5
Atworth 8 A3
Auchduart 52 H2
Auchenblae 51 J6
Auchencairn 35 H8
Auchengray 40 H3
Auchertool 40 D5
Auchinleck 34 A6
Auchronie 51 J3
Auchterarder 45 H11
Auchterderran 40 D5
Auchtermuchty 40 B5
Auchtertyre 47 J8
Audlem 20 B7
Audley 21 A8
Auldearn 49 C10
Aultbea 46 C8
Austwick 31 H13
Aveton Gifford ...3 G14
Aviemore 49 G9
Avoch 48 C8
Avonmouth 14 J4
Axbridge 7 F13
Axminster 4 D6
Axmouth 4 E6
Aylesbury 16 D3
Aylesford 11 D8
Aylesham 11 D13
Aylsham 24 C6
Aynho 15 C14
Ayr 34 A4
Aysgarth 32 F1

Ayton
 Borders 41 G12
 N Yorks 33 F11

B

Bac 55 C6
Backwell 7 E13
Bacton 24 B8
Bacup 27 C9
Badenscoth 50 D6
Badenyon 50 F2
Badminton 14 H7
Badrallach 52 J2
Bagh a Chaisteil /
 Castlebay 54 K3
Bagillt 26 H3
Bagshot 16 J4
Baildon 27 B12
Baile Ailein 55 E5
Baile Mhartainn ..54 B4
Bainbridge 32 E1
Bainton 33 J11
Bakewell 27 J13
Bala 18 G9
Balbeggie 45 F13
Balblair 49 B8
Balcombe 10 G4
Balderton 28 J7
Balephuil 42 D1
Balfour 56 E4
Balfron 39 B10
Balintore 49 A9
Ballachulish 44 D2
Ballantrae 34 E2
Ballasalla 30 H2
Ballater 51 H2
Ballaugh 30 F3
Ballinaby 43 M4
Ballinluig 45 D11
Balloch
 Highland 49 D8
 W Dunb 39 B8
Ballochan 51 H4
Ballygrant 43 M5
Ballyhaugh 42 C3
Balmacara 47 J8
Balmaclellan 34 F7
Balmedie 50 F8
Balnacoil 53 H10
Balnapaling 49 B8
Balquhidder 44 G7
Balsall 21 J13
Baltasound 57 A7
Balvicar 42 G9
Bamber Bridge ...26 C6
Bamburgh 41 K14
Bamford 27 G13
Bampton
 Devon 4 A3
 Oxon 15 F12
Banbury 15 C13
Banchory 51 H5
Banff 50 A5
Bangor 18 C5
Bangor-is-y-coed .20 B5
Banham 24 G5
Bankend 35 G11
Bankfoot 45 F12
Bankhead 50 F7
Banks 26 C4
Bannockburn 39 A13
Banstead 10 D3
Banwell 7 F12
Barabhas 55 B5
Barassie 39 G8
Barbon 31 F12
Bardney 29 H10
Bardon 22 J1
Bargoed 7 B10
Bargrennan 34 F4
Barham 11 E13
Bar Hill 23 J2
Barkway 17 B8
Barlaston 28 G3
Barlby 28 A5

Barley 17 B9
Barmby Moor 33 K9
Barmoor Castle ...41 J12
Barmouth 19 J6
Barnard Castle ...32 C2
Barnet 16 F7
Barnetby le Wold .29 D9
Barnham 24 H3
Barnhill 49 C12
Barnoldswick 27 A9
Barnsley 28 D2
Barnstaple 6 H4
Barnt Green 21 J11
Barr 34 D3
Barrhead 39 E9
Barrhill 34 E3
Barrowford 27 B9
Barrow-in-Furness .30 G7
Barrow upon
 Humber 29 B9
Barry
 Angus 51 P4
 V Glam 7 E10
Barton 32 D4
Barton-le-Clay ...16 C5
Barton upon
 Humber 29 B9
Barwell 22 F3
Baschurch 20 D5
Basildon 17 G12
Basingstoke 9 B11
Baslow 27 H13
Baston 23 D10
Bath 8 A2
Bathford 8 A2
Bathgate 40 G2
Batley 27 C13
Battle 11 H8
Bawdeswell 24 C5
Bawtry 28 E5
Bayston Hill 20 F5
Beachley 14 G4
Beaconsfield 16 G4
Beadnell 37 A11
Beaminster 5 D8
Bearsden 39 C10
Bearsted 11 D8
Beattock 35 C11
Beaufort 13 E15
Beaulieu 9 G8
Beauly 48 D6
Beaumaris 18 C5
Bebington 26 G4
Beccles 24 F9
Beckermet 30 D6
Beckfoot 35 J11
Beckhampton 15 K10
Beckingham 28 E6
Beckington 8 B3
Beck Row 24 H1
Bedale 32 F4
Beddgelert 18 F5
Bedford 16 A5
Bedlington 37 E11
Bedwas 7 C10
Bedworth 22 G2
Beeford 33 J13
Beer 4 E6
Beeston 22 B4
Beeswing 35 G9
Begelly 12 F5
Beguildy 20 J3
Beighton 28 F3
Beith 39 E8
Belbroughton 21 J10
Belchford 29 G11
Belford 41 K14
Bellingham 36 E7
Bellsbank 34 C5
Bellshill 39 D12
Belmont
 Blackburn 26 D7
 Shetland 57 B6
Belper 28 K2
Belsay 37 F9

Beltinge 11 C12
Belton
  N Lincs 28 D6
  Norf 24 E9
Bembridge. 9 J11
Benington 23 A12
Benllech. 18 B5
Benson 16 F1
Bentley
  Hants 9 C12
  S Yorks 28 D4
Benwick 23 F12
Bere Alston 3 E12
Bere Regis 8 H3
Berkeley 14 G5
Berkhamsted. 16 E4
Berriedale 53 F13
Berriew. 20 F2
Berrow 7 F11
Berwick 10 J6
Berwick-upon-
  Tweed. 41 H12
Bethersden 11 F10
Bethesda. 18 D6
Bettws Bledrws 19 Q6
Bettyhill 53 B9
Betws 13 H13
Betws-y-Coed 18 E7
Beulah 13 A13
Beverley 29 A9
Bewcastle 36 F4
Bewdley 21 J8
Bexhill. 11 J8
Bexley 10 B5
Bibury 15 F10
Bicester 15 D14
Bickington 4 F1
Bicton. 20 E5
Biddenden 11 F9
Biddulph. 27 K9
Bideford 6 J3
Bidford-on-Avon 15 A10
Bigbury on Sea 3 G14
Biggar. 40 K3
Biggin Hill 10 D5
Biggleswade 16 A7
Bildeston 25 L4
Billericay 17 F11
Billesdon 22 E6
Billingborough 23 B10
Billingham. 32 B6
Billinghay. 29 J10
Billingshurst 10 G1
Bilston 21 G10
Binbrook 29 E11
Bingham. 22 B5
Bingley 27 B12
Birchgrove. 13 G10
Birchington 11 C14
Birdlip. 15 E8
Birkdale. 26 D4
Birkenhead 26 G4
Birmingham 21 H11
Birtley
  Northumb. 36 F7
  T&W. 37 H11
Bishop Auckland 32 B4
Bishopbriggs. 39 C11
Bishop Monkton. 32 H5
Bishop's Castle. 20 H4
Bishop's Cleeve 15 D8
Bishop's Frome 14 B5
Bishops Lydeard 7 J10
Bishop's Nympton 6 J6
Bishop's Stortford . . .17 C9
Bishop's Tawton 6 J4
Bishopsteignton 4 F3
Bishopstoke. 9 F9
Bishopston 13 H9
Bishop's Waltham 9 F10
Bitton 14 K5
Blaby 22 F4
Blackburn 26 C7
Blackfield. 9 G9
Blackford
  Cumb 36 G2

Blackford *continued*
  Perth 45 J11
Blackpool. 26 B4
Blackridge. 39 D13
Blackwall Tunnel 10 B4
Blackwaterfoot. 38 H4
Blackwood
  Caerph 7 B10
  S Lanark 39 F12
Blaenau Ffestiniog . . .18 F7
Blaenavon 14 F1
Blaengraw 13 G13
Blagdon 7 F14
Blaina 7 A11
Blair Atholl 45 C10
Blairgowrie 45 E13
Blakeney
  Glos 14 F5
  Norf 24 A5
Blanchand 37 H8
Blandford Forum 8 G3
Blaydon 37 G10
Bleadon 7 F12
Blean. 11 D12
Bletchingdon 15 E14
Bletchley 16 B3
Blewbury 15 H14
Blidworth. 28 J5
Blindburn. 36 B7
Blisworth 22 K6
Blockley 15 C10
Blofield. 24 D8
Bloxham 15 C13
Blubberhouses 32 J3
Blundeston 24 F10
Blyth
  Northumb 37 E12
  Notts 28 F5
Blyth Bridge 40 J4
Blythburgh. 25 H9
Blythe Bridge 21 B10
Blyton 28 E7
Boath 48 A6
Boat of Garten 49 G10
Boddam
  Aberds 50 C10
  Shetland. 57 L5
Bodedern. 18 C3
Bodenham 14 A4
Bodiam. 11 G8
Bodinnick 3 F9
Bodmin 3 E8
Bognor Regis 9 H14
Boldon 37 G12
Bollington 27 H10
Bolney. 10 G3
Bolsover 28 G3
Bolton. 27 E8
Bolton Abbey 32 J2
Bolton Bridge 32 J2
Bolton by Bowland .31 K13
Bolton le Sands 31 H10
Bonarbridge 52 J8
Bonawe 44 F2
Bonby 29 C8
Bonchester Bridge . . .36 B4
Bonchurch. 9 K10
Bo'ness. 40 E2
Bonhill 39 B9
Bonnybridge 39 B13
Bonnyrigg 40 G6
Bonvilston 7 D9
Boot 30 D7
Bootle
  Cumb 30 F7
  Mers. 26 F4
Bordon 9 D13
Borehamwood 16 F6
Boreland 35 D12
Borgh 55 B6
Borgue 34 J7
Boroughbridge. 32 H5
Borough Green 10 D7
Borrowdale 31 C8
Borth 19 M6
Bosbury 14 B6
Boscastle 3 C8
Bosham 9 G13
Boston 23 A12

Boston Spa 32 K6
Botesdale. 24 H5
Bothel 35 J12
Bothenhampton 5 E8
Botley 15 F13
Bottesford 22 B7
Bottisham 23 J14
Botwnnog 18 G2
Boughton 28 H5
Bourne 23 C9
Bourne End 16 G4
Bournemouth 8 H5
Bourton-on-the-
  Water 15 D10
Bovey Tracey 4 F2
Bow 4 D1
Bowes 32 C2
Bowmore 43 N5
Bowness-on-
  Solway 35 G13
Bowness-on-
  Windermere 31 E10
Box. 14 K7
Bozeat. 23 K8
Brabourne 11 E11
Brabourne Lees 11 F11
Bracadale. 47 H3
Bracebridge Heath . .29 H8
Bracklesham 9 H13
Brackley
  Northants. 15 C15
  Northants. 16 B1
Bracknell 16 J3
Braco 45 J10
Bradford. 27 B12
Bradford-on-Avon. . . .8 A3
Brading 9 J11
Bradpole 5 D8
Bradwell Waterside. .25 Q5
Bradworthy 6 K2
Brae. 57 F4
Braeantra. 48 A6
Braemar. 49 J12
Braemore
  Highland. 48 A3
  Highland. 53 F12
Brae Roy Lodge 48 J4
Brailsford. 21 B13
Braintree 17 C12
Bramford 25 L6
Bramhall 27 G9
Bramhope. 27 A13
Brampton
  Cambs 23 H11
  Cumb 36 G4
Brancaster. 24 A2
Branderburgh. 49 A13
Brandon
  Durham 37 J11
  Suff. 24 G2
Branston. 29 H9
Brantham 25 M6
Bratton Fleming 6 H5
Braunston 22 J4
Braunton 6 H3
Bray. 16 H4
Breage 2 J4
Breakish 47 J6
Bream 14 F5
Breanais 55 E2
Brechfa 13 C9
Brechin 51 L5
Breck of Cruan 56 E3
Brecon 13 D14
Brede 11 H9
Bredenbury 14 A5
Bremirehoull. 57 K5
Brent 10 A3
Brentwood. 17 F11
Bretforton 15 B9
Brewood 21 F9
Bride 30 E4
Bridestowe 3 C13
Bridge. 11 D12
Bridgend
  Argyll 43 M5
  Bridgend. 13 J13
Bridge of Allan 39 A12
Bridge of Balgie 44 E7

Bridge of Cally 45 D13
Bridge of Don 50 F8
Bridge of Earn 45 H13
Bridge of Orchy 44 E5
Bridge of Weir 39 D8
Bridgnorth. 21 G8
Bridgwater 7 H12
Bridlington 33 H13
Bridport 5 D8
Brierfield 27 B9
Brierley Hill 21 H10
Brigg 29 D9
Brighouse 27 C12
Brighstone. 9 J9
Brightlingsea 25 P5
Brighton 10 J4
Brigstock 23 G8
Brill 16 D1
Brimfield 20 K6
Brinian 56 D4
Brinklow. 22 H3
Brinkworth 15 H9
Bristol 14 J4
Briston 24 B5
Briton Ferry. 13 G11
Brixham 4 H3
Brixton 3 F13
Brixworth. 22 H6
Brize Norton 15 F11
Broad Chalke 8 E5
Broadclyst 4 D3
Broadford. 47 J6
Broad Haven 12 E2
Broadhembury 4 C4
Broad Hinton. 15 J10
Broadmayne 5 E11
Broadstairs 11 C15
Broadstone 8 H4
Broadwas 14 A6
Broadway. 15 C10
Broadwey. 5 E10
Broadwindsor 5 C8
Brochel 46 G5
Brockenhurst 9 G8
Brockworth 15 E8
Brocton 21 E10
Brodick. 38 G5
Bromfield 20 J5
Bromham
  Bedford 23 K8
  Wilts. 8 A4
Bromley 10 C5
Bromley Green 11 F10
Brompton. 32 E5
Brompton Regis 4 A3
Bromsgrove. 21 J10
Bromyard 14 A5
Brooke 24 F7
Broomfield. 17 D12
Broomhaugh 37 G9
Broomhill. 37 C11
Brora 53 H10
Broseley. 20 F7
Brothertoft 29 K11
Brotton 33 B8
Brough
  Cumb 31 C14
  E Yorks 29 B8
  Highland. 53 A14
  Shetland. 57 E5
Broughton
  Borders 40 K4
  Hants 8 E6
  Lancs 26 B6
  N Lincs 29 D8
  Northants. 22 H7
Broughton Astley. . . .22 F4
Broughton-in-
  Furness 31 F8
Broughty Ferry 51 P3
Brownhills 21 F11
Broxburn 40 F3
Broxton. 20 A5
Bruichladdich 43 M4
Brundall 24 E8
Brunton
  Northumb. 37 A11
  Northumb. 37 F8
Bruton 8 D1

Brymbo. 20 A3
Brynamman 13 E11
Bryncrug 19 K5
Brynmawr 13 E15
Brynsiencyn. 18 D4
Bubwith 28 A6
Buchlyvie 39 A10
Buckden
  Cambs 23 J10
  N Yorks. 32 G1
Buckfast. 4 G1
Buckfastleigh 4 G1
Buckhaven. 40 D6
Buckie. 50 A3
Buckingham 16 B2
Buckland 15 G12
Buckland Brewer 6 K3
Buckland Newton . . .5 C10
Buckley. 26 J3
Bucksburn 50 F8
Buck's Cross 6 J2
Bude 3 A10
Budleigh Salterton . . .4 E4
Bugbrooke. 22 K5
Bugle. 3 F8
Builth Wells 13 A14
Bulford 8 C6
Bulkington 22 G2
Bulwell 22 A4
Bunbury 26 K6
Bunessan 42 F5
Bungay 24 G8
Bunnahabhain 43 L6
Buntingford. 17 C8
Bunwell 24 F6
Burbage
  Derbys 27 H11
  Leics. 22 F3
  Wilts. 8 B7
Bures. 25 M4
Burford 15 E11
Burgess Hill. 10 H4
Burgh-by-Sands 36 H2
Burghclere. 9 A9
Burghead 49 B12
Burghfield Common . 16 J1
Burgh le Marsh. 29 H14
Burley
  Hants 8 G7
  W Yorks 32 K3
Burlton 20 D5
Burneside 31 E11
Burness 56 B6
Burnham 16 G4
Burnham Market 24 A3
Burnham-on-
  Crouch 17 F14
Burnham-on-Sea 7 G12
Burniston 33 E12
Burnley 27 B9
Burnmouth 41 G12
Burntisland 40 E5
Burntwood. 21 F11
Burrafirth. 57 A7
Burravoe 57 D6
Burrelton 45 F14
Burry Port
  Carms. 12 G4
  Carms. 13 G5
Burscough Bridge . . .26 D5
Burstwick. 29 B11
Burton. 31 G11
Burton Agnes 33 H13
Burton Bradstock. . . .5 E8
Burton Fleming 33 G12
Burton in Lonsdale .31 G12
Burton Latimer 22 H7
Burton upon Stather 28 C7
Burton upon Trent . .21 D13
Burwash 10 G7
Burwell 23 J14
Burwick 56 H4
Bury 27 E9
Bury St Edmunds . . .25 J3
Bushey 16 F6
Buttermere 30 C7
Buxted. 10 G6
Buxton 27 H11
Byfield. 15 A14

Byfleet . . . 16 J5
Bylchau . . . 18 D9

C

Cabrach . . . 50 E2
Caenby Corner . . . 29 F8
Caergwrle . . . 20 A4
Caerleon . . . 7 C12
Caernarfon . . . 18 D4
Caerphilly . . . 7 C10
Caersws . . . 19 L10
Caerwent . . . 14 G3
Cairinis . . . 54 C5
Cairndow . . . 44 H3
Cairngaan . . . 34 K2
Cairnryan . . . 34 G1
Caister-on-Sea . . . 24 D10
Caistor . . . 29 D10
Calanais . . . 55 D4
Caldbeck . . . 36 J2
Calder Bridge . . . 30 D6
Caldercruix . . . 39 D13
Caldicot . . . 14 H3
Calfsound . . . 56 C5
Calgary . . . 42 C5
Callander . . . 45 J8
Callington . . . 3 E11
Calne . . . 15 J9
Calshot . . . 9 H9
Calstock . . . 3 E12
Calverton . . . 28 K5
Cam . . . 14 G6
Camber . . . 11 H10
Camberley . . . 16 K3
Cambo . . . 37 E9
Camborne . . . 2 H4
Cambourne . . . 23 K12
Cambridge . . . 23 K13
Camden . . . 10 A3
Camelford . . . 3 C9
Cammachmore . . . 51 H8
Campbeltown . . . 38 H2
Camrose . . . 12 E3
Canisbay . . . 53 A15
Cannich . . . 48 E4
Cannington . . . 7 H11
Cannock . . . 21 F10
Canonbie . . . 36 F2
Canterbury . . . 11 D12
Cantley . . . 24 E8
Canvey Island . . . 17 G13
Caol . . . 44 B3
Caolas Stocinis . . . 55 H3
Caoles . . . 42 D2
Capel . . . 10 F2
Capel Curig . . . 18 E7
Capel St Mary . . . 25 M6
Carbis Bay . . . 2 H3
Carbost
  Highland . . . 46 G4
  Highland . . . 47 H3
Cardiff . . . 7 D10
Cardigan . . . 12 B5
Cardington . . . 16 A5
Cardross . . . 39 C8
Cargill . . . 45 F13
Carhampton . . . 7 G9
Carisbrooke . . . 9 J9
Cark . . . 31 G9
Carlabhagh . . . 55 C4
Carleton Rode . . . 24 F6
Carlisle . . . 36 H3
Carlops . . . 40 H4
Carlton
  Notts . . . 22 A5
  N Yorks . . . 28 B5
Carlton Colville . . . 24 G10
Carlton-in-Lindrick . 28 F4
Carlton Miniott . . . 32 E4
Carluke . . . 39 E13
Carmarthen . . . 12 E8
Carmyllie . . . 51 N4
Carnachuin . . . 49 J9
Carnforth . . . 31 G11
Carno . . . 19 L9
Carnoustie . . . 51 P4
Carnwath . . . 40 J2

Carradale . . . 38 G3
Carrbridge . . . 49 F10
Carrick . . . 38 A7
Carronbridge . . . 35 D9
Carsaig . . . 42 F7
Carskiey . . . 38 K1
Carsphairn . . . 34 D6
Carstairs . . . 40 J2
Carterton . . . 15 F11
Cartmel . . . 31 G9
Castle Acre . . . 24 D3
Castlebay / Bagh a
  Chaisteil . . . 54 K3
Castle Cary . . . 8 D1
Castle Donington . . 22 C3
Castle Douglas . . . 35 G8
Castleford . . . 28 B3
Castlemartin . . . 12 G3
Castleside . . . 37 J9
Castleton
  Derbys . . . 27 G12
  N Yorks . . . 33 D8
Castletown
  Highland . . . 53 B14
  IoM . . . 30 J2
Caston . . . 24 F4
Castor . . . 23 F10
Catcleugh . . . 36 C6
Caterham . . . 10 D4
Caton . . . 31 H11
Catrine . . . 39 H10
Catsfield . . . 11 H8
Catterall . . . 26 A6
Catterick . . . 32 E4
Catterick Camp . . . 32 E3
Catton . . . 36 H7
Caulkerbush . . . 35 H10
Cawdor . . . 49 C9
Cawood . . . 28 A4
Cawston . . . 24 C6
Caythorpe . . . 29 K8
Ceann Tarabhaigh . . 55 F4
Cefn-mawr . . . 20 B3
Cemaes . . . 18 A3
Cemmaes Road . . . 19 K8
Cenarth . . . 12 B6
Ceres . . . 40 B7
Cerne Abbas . . . 5 C10
Cerrigydrudion . . . 18 F9
Chacewater . . . 2 G5
Chaddesley Corbet . . 21 J9
Chadwell St Mary . . 17 H11
Chagford . . . 3 C14
Chalfont St Giles . . 16 F4
Chalford . . . 15 F8
Chalgrove . . . 16 F1
Challacombe . . . 6 H5
Challock . . . 11 E11
Chandler's Ford . . . 9 E9
Channel Tunnel . . . 11 F12
Chapel en le Frith . . 27 G11
Chapel St Leonards 29 G14
Chapeltown
  S Lanark . . . 39 F11
  S Yorks . . . 28 E2
Chard . . . 4 C7
Charing . . . 11 E10
Charlbury . . . 15 E12
Charlestown of
  Aberlour . . . 49 D13
Charlton . . . 15 H8
Charlton Horethorne 5 A10
Charlton Kings . . . 15 E8
Charlwood . . . 10 E3
Charminster . . . 5 D10
Charmouth . . . 4 D7
Chartham . . . 11 D12
Chatham . . . 17 J12
Chathill . . . 37 A10
Chatteris . . . 23 G12
Chatton . . . 37 A9
Chawleigh . . . 4 C1
Cheadle
  Grt Manchester . . 27 G9
  Staffs . . . 21 B11
Chedburgh . . . 25 K2
Cheddar . . . 7 F13
Cheddleton . . . 21 A10
Chellaston . . . 22 B2

Chelmarsh . . . 21 H8
Chelmsford . . . 17 E12
Cheltenham . . . 15 D8
Chepstow . . . 14 G4
Cherhill . . . 15 K9
Cheriton . . . 9 E11
Cheriton Fitzpaine . . 4 C2
Chertsey . . . 16 J5
Chesham . . . 16 E4
Cheshunt . . . 17 E8
Chester . . . 26 J5
Chesterfield . . . 28 G2
Chester-le-Street . . 37 H11
Chew Magna . . . 7 E14
Chewton Mendip . . 7 F14
Chichester . . . 9 G13
Chiddingfold . . . 9 D14
Chideock . . . 5 D8
Chigwell . . . 17 F9
Chilcompton . . . 8 B1
Chilham . . . 11 D11
Chillington . . . 4 J1
Chilton . . . 32 A4
Chingford . . . 17 F8
Chinnor . . . 16 E2
Chippenham . . . 15 J8
Chipping Campden . 15 C10
Chipping Norton . . 15 D12
Chipping Ongar . . 17 E10
Chipping Sodbury . . 14 H6
Chirbury . . . 20 G3
Chirk . . . 20 C3
Chirnside . . . 41 H11
Chiseldon . . . 15 J10
Chitterne . . . 8 C4
Chobham . . . 16 J4
Chollerton . . . 37 F8
Chorley . . . 26 D6
Chorleywood . . . 16 F5
Christchurch
  Cambs . . . 23 F13
  Dorset . . . 8 H6
Christow . . . 4 E2
Chudleigh . . . 4 F2
Chulmleigh . . . 6 K5
Churchdown . . . 14 E7
Churchill . . . 15 D11
Churchstow . . . 4 J1
Church Stretton . . 20 G5
Church Village . . . 7 C9
Chwilog . . . 18 G4
Cilgerran . . . 12 B5
Cille Bhrighde . . . 54 H4
Cilycwm . . . 13 C11
Cinderford . . . 14 E5
Cirencester . . . 15 F9
City of London . . 10 A4
Clachan
  Argyll . . . 38 G2
  Highland . . . 47 H5
Clachan na Luib . . 54 C5
Clackmannan . . . 40 D2
Clacton-on-Sea . . 25 P6
Cladich . . . 44 G2
Claggan . . . 42 D9
Claigan . . . 46 F2
Clanfield . . . 9 F13
Claonaig . . . 38 E3
Clapham
  Bedford . . . 23 K9
  N Yorks . . . 31 H13
Clare . . . 25 L2
Clashmore . . . 53 K9
Clavering . . . 17 C9
Claverley . . . 21 G8
Clawton . . . 3 B11
Clay Cross . . . 28 H2
Claydon . . . 25 K6
Claypole . . . 28 K7
Cleadale . . . 47 N4
Cleat . . . 56 H4
Cleator Moor . . . 30 C6
Cleethorpes . . . 29 D11
Cleeve Prior . . . 15 A10
Clehonger . . . 14 C3
Cleobury Mortimer . 20 J7
Clevedon . . . 7 D13
Cleveleys . . . 26 A4

Cley . . . 24 A5
Cliffe . . . 17 H12
Clifford . . . 14 B1
Clipston . . . 22 G6
Clipstone . . . 28 H4
Clitheroe . . . 27 A8
Clive . . . 20 D6
Clophill . . . 16 B5
Closeburn . . . 35 D9
Cloughton . . . 33 E12
Clova . . . 51 K2
Clovelly . . . 6 J2
Clovenfords . . . 40 K7
Clowne . . . 28 G3
Clun . . . 20 H4
Clunbury . . . 20 H4
Clunes . . . 48 K3
Clungunford . . . 20 J4
Clutton . . . 8 B1
Clydach . . . 13 F10
Clydebank . . . 39 D10
Clynnog-fawr . . . 18 F4
Clyro . . . 14 B1
Coalbrookdale . . . 20 F7
Coalburn . . . 39 G13
Coalville . . . 22 D3
Coatbridge . . . 39 D12
Cobham
  Kent . . . 17 J11
  Sur . . . 10 D2
Cock Bridge . . . 49 G13
Cockburnspath . . 41 F10
Cockenzie . . . 40 F7
Cockerham . . . 31 J10
Cockermouth . . . 30 A7
Cockfield
  Durham . . . 32 B3
  Suff. . . . 25 K4
Cockshutt . . . 20 D5
Coddenham . . . 25 K6
Codford St Mary . . 8 D4
Coggeshall . . . 25 N3
Coignafearn Lodge . 48 G7
Coille Mhorgil . . . 48 H1
Coillore . . . 47 H3
Colby . . . 30 J2
Colchester . . . 25 N5
Cold Ashton . . . 14 J6
Coldingham . . . 41 G12
Coldstream . . . 41 J11
Coleford
  Devon . . . 4 D1
  Glos . . . 14 F4
Coleshill . . . 21 H13
Colinton . . . 40 G5
Colintraive . . . 38 C5
Collieston . . . 50 E9
Collin . . . 35 F11
Collingbourne
  Kingston . . . 8 B7
Collingham
  Notts . . . 28 H7
  W Yorks . . . 32 K5
Colmonell . . . 34 E2
Colne . . . 27 B10
Colpy . . . 50 D5
Colsterworth . . . 23 C8
Coltishall . . . 24 C7
Colwall . . . 37 F8
Colwich . . . 21 D11
Colwyn Bay . . . 18 C8
Colyton . . . 4 D6
Combe Martin . . . 6 G4
Comberton . . . 23 K12
Combwich . . . 7 G11
Compton
  W Berks . . . 15 J14
  W Sus. . . . 9 F12
Compton Martin . . 7 F14
Comrie . . . 45 G9
Condover . . . 20 F5
Congleton . . . 27 J9
Congresbury . . . 7 E13
Coningsby . . . 29 J11
Conisbrough . . . 28 E4
Coniston . . . 31 E8
Connah's Quay . . 26 J3
Connel . . . 44 F1
Connel Park . . . 34 B7

Cononbridge . . . 48 C6
Consett . . . 37 H10
Contin . . . 48 C5
Conwy . . . 18 C7
Cookham . . . 16 G4
Coolham . . . 10 G2
Coombe Bissett . . 8 E6
Copplestone . . . 4 C1
Coppull . . . 26 D6
Copthorne . . . 10 F4
Corbridge . . . 37 G8
Corby . . . 22 G7
Corby Glen . . . 23 C9
Corfe Castle . . . 8 J4
Corfe Mullen . . . 8 H4
Cornhill on Tweed . 41 K11
Corpach . . . 44 B2
Corran . . . 44 C2
Corrie . . . 38 F5
Corringham
  Lincs . . . 28 E7
  Thurrock . . . 17 G12
Corris . . . 19 K7
Corsham . . . 14 J7
Corsley . . . 8 C3
Corsock . . . 35 F8
Corton . . . 24 F10
Corwen . . . 18 F10
Coryton . . . 17 G12
Coseley . . . 21 G10
Cosham . . . 9 G11
Costessey . . . 24 D6
Cotgrave . . . 22 B5
Cotherstone . . . 32 B2
Cottenham . . . 23 J13
Cottered . . . 17 C8
Cottesmore . . . 23 D8
Cottingham . . . 29 A9
Coulags . . . 46 G9
Coulport . . . 38 B7
Countesthorpe . . 22 F4
Coupar Angus . . 45 E14
Cove
  Argyll . . . 38 B7
  Highland . . . 46 B8
Cove Bay . . . 50 G8
Coventry . . . 22 H2
Coverack . . . 2 K5
Cowbit . . . 23 D11
Cowbridge . . . 13 J13
Cowdenbeath . . 40 D4
Cowes . . . 9 H9
Cowfold . . . 10 G3
Cowpen . . . 37 E11
Cowplain . . . 9 F11
Coxheath . . . 11 D8
Coylton . . . 34 A5
Craggie . . . 49 E8
Crai . . . 13 D12
Craibstone . . . 50 B3
Craigellachie . . . 49 D13
Craighouse . . . 43 M7
Craigmore . . . 38 D6
Craignure . . . 42 E9
Craigtown . . . 53 C11
Crail . . . 41 C9
Cramlington . . . 37 F11
Cranborne . . . 8 F5
Cranbrook . . . 11 F8
Cranleigh . . . 10 F1
Cranmore . . . 8 C1
Cranstal . . . 30 E4
Cranwell . . . 29 K9
Crathie . . . 49 J13
Craven Arms . . . 20 H5
Crawford . . . 35 A10
Crawfordjohn . . 39 H13
Crawley . . . 10 F3
Creag Ghoraidh . . 54 E5
Creake . . . 24 B3
Credenhill . . . 14 B3
Crediton . . . 4 D2
Creetown . . . 34 H5
Cressage . . . 20 F7
Cresselly . . . 12 F4
Crewe . . . 21 A8

Crewkerne 5 C8
Crianlarich 44 G5
Criccieth 18 G5
Crick 22 H4
Crickhowell 14 E1
Cricklade 15 G10
Crieff 45 G10
Crimond 50 B9
Crinan 38 A2
Crocketford 35 F9
Croggan 42 F9
Croglin 36 J4
Croick 52 J6
Cromarty 49 B8
Cromer 24 A7
Cromor 55 E6
Crondall 9 C12
Crook 37 K10
Crookham 41 K12
Crooklands 31 F11
Crosbost 55 E6
Crosby 35 J11
Crosby
  Ravensworth 31 C12
Cross-Hands 13 E9
Crosshill 34 C4
Crossmichael 35 G8
Croston 26 D5
Crowborough 10 F6
Crowland 23 D11
Crowle 28 C6
Crowthorne 16 J3
Croxton Kerrial 22 C7
Croyde 6 H3
Croydon 10 C4
Cruden Bay 50 D9
Crudgington 20 E7
Crulabhig 55 D3
Crymych 12 C5
Cuaig 46 F7
Cuan 42 G9
Cuckfield 10 G4
Cuddington
  Bucks 16 D2
  Ches W 26 H6
Cudworth 28 C2
Cuffley 17 E8
Culgaith 31 A12
Culkein 52 E2
Cullen 50 A4
Cullicudden 48 B7
Cullivoe 57 B6
Culloden 49 D8
Cullompton 4 C4
Culmazie 34 H4
Culmington 20 H5
Culmstock 4 B5
Culrain 52 J7
Cults 50 G7
Cumbernauld 39 C12
Cuminestown 50 B7
Cummertrees 35 G12
Cumnock 34 A6
Cumnor 15 F13
Cumwhinton 36 H3
Cupar 40 B6
Currie 40 G4
Curry Rivel 7 J12
Cwmafan 13 G11
Cwmann 13 B9
Cwmbran 7 B11
Cwrt 19 K7
Cymmer 13 G12
Cynwyl Elfed 12 D7

D

Dagenham 17 G10
Dail bho Dheas 55 A6
Dailly 34 C3
Dalabrog 54 G4
Dalbeattie 35 G9
Dale 12 F2
Dale of Walls 57 G2
Dalguise 45 E11

Dalhalvaig 53 C11
Dalkeith 40 G6
Dallas 49 C12
Dalleagles 34 B6
Dalmally 44 G3
Dalmellington 34 C5
Dalnaspidal 45 B8
Dalnessie 52 G8
Dalry 38 F7
Dalrymple 34 B4
Dalston 36 H2
Dalton
  Dumfries 35 F12
  Northumb 37 H8
  N Yorks 32 D5
Dalton-in-Furness . . .31 G8
Dalwhinnie 45 A8
Damerham 8 F6
Danbury 17 E13
Darlington 32 C4
Dartford 17 H10
Dartford Crossing . .17 H10
Dartington 4 G1
Dartmouth 4 H2
Darton 28 C2
Darvel 39 G10
Darwen 26 C7
Daventry 22 J4
Davington 35 C13
Dawlish 4 F3
Deal 11 D14
Dearham 35 K11
Dearne 28 D3
Debenham 25 J6
Deddington 15 C13
Deeping St
  Nicholas 23 D11
Deerness 56 F5
Deganwy 18 C7
Delabole 3 C8
Delchirach 49 E12
Delves 37 H10
Denbigh 18 D10
Denby Dale 27 E13
Denholm 36 B4
Denny 39 B13
Dent 31 F13
Denton
  Grt Manchester 27 F10
  Lincs 22 B7
Derby 22 B2
Dereham 24 D4
Dersingham 24 B1
Dervaig 42 C6
Desborough 22 G6
Desford 22 E3
Devil's Bridge 19 N7
Devizes 8 A5
Devonport 3 F12
Dewsbury 27 C13
Diabaig 46 E8
Dibden Purlieu 9 G9
Dickleborough 24 G6
Didcot 15 H14
Digby 29 J9
Dinas Mawddwy 19 J8
Dinas Powis 7 D10
Dingwall 48 C6
Dinnington 28 F4
Dinton 8 D5
Dippen 38 H5
Dirleton 41 E8
Diss 24 G6
Distington 30 B6
Ditchingham 24 F8
Ditchling 10 H4
Dittisham 4 H2
Ditton Priors 20 H7
Dobwalls 3 E10
Docking 24 B2
Dockray 31 B9
Doddinghurst 17 F10
Doddington
  Cambs 23 F12
  Northumb 41 K12
Dolanog 20 E1
Dolfor 20 H2
Dolgarrog 18 D7
Dolgellau 19 J7

Dollar 40 D2
Dolphinton 40 J4
Dolton 6 K4
Dolwyddelan 18 E7
Doncaster 28 D4
Donhead StAndrew . . 8 E4
Donington 23 B11
Donnington 21 E8
Dorchester
  Dorset 5 E10
  Oxon 15 G14
Dores 48 E7
Dorking 10 E2
Dornie 47 J8
Dornoch 53 K9
Dorridge 21 J12
Dorstone 14 B2
Douglas
  IoM 30 H3
  S Lanark 39 G13
Dounby 56 D2
Doune 45 J9
Dounreay 53 B11
Dove Holes 27 H11
Dover 11 E14
Doveridge 21 C12
Downham 23 G14
Downham Market . . .24 E1
Downton 8 E6
Drayton 24 D6
Dreghorn 39 G8
Drem 41 F8
Driffield 33 J12
Drigg 30 D6
Drimnin 42 C7
Droitwich Spa 21 K10
Dronfield 28 G2
Drongan 34 B5
Druid 18 F10
Drumbeg 52 E3
Drumgask 48 J7
Drumjohn 34 D6
Drummore 34 K2
Drumnadrochit 48 E6
Drymen 39 B9
Drynoch 47 H4
Duchally 52 G5
Duddington 23 E8
Dudley 21 G10
Duffield 22 A2
Dufftown 50 D2
Dukinfield 27 F10
Dullingham 25 K1
Dulnain Bridge 49 F10
Duloe 3 F10
Dulverton 4 A3
Dumbarton 39 C9
Dumfries 35 F10
Dunans 38 A5
Dunbar 41 F9
Dunbeath 53 F13
Dunblane 45 J9
Dunchurch 22 H3
Dundee 51 P2
Dundonald 39 G8
Dundrennan 35 J8
Dunecht 50 G6
Dunfermline 40 E4
Dungraggan 44 J7
Dunino 41 B8
Dunipace 39 B13
Dunkeld 45 E12
Dunlop 39 F9
Dunnet 53 B14
Dunning 45 H12
Dunnington 33 J8
Dunoon 38 C6
Dunragit 34 H2
Duns 41 H10
Dunsby 23 C10
Dunscore 35 E9
Dunsford 4 E2
Dunstable 16 C5
Dunster 7 G8
Dunston 21 E10
Dunsyre 40 J3
Dunure 34 B3
Dunvegan 46 G2
Dunwich 25 J9

Durham 37 J11
Durness 52 B6
Durrington 8 C6
Dursley 14 G6
Dyce 50 F7
Dykehead 51 L2
Dymchurch 11 G12
Dymock 14 C5
Dysart 40 D6
Dyserth 26 H1

E

Eaglescliffe 32 C6
Eaglesfield 35 F13
Eaglesham 39 E10
Eakring 28 H5
Ealing 10 B2
Earby 27 A10
Eardisley 14 B2
Earith 23 H12
Earls Barton 22 J7
Earl's Colne 25 N3
Earlsferry 41 C8
Earl Shilton 22 F3
Earl Soham 25 J7
Earlston 41 K8
Earsdon 37 F12
Easdale 42 G9
Easebourne 9 E14
Easington
  Durham 37 J13
  E Yorks 29 C12
Easington Colliery . . .37 J13
Easingwold 32 G7
East Bergholt 25 M5
East Boldre 9 H8
Eastbourne 10 K7
East Brent 7 F12
East Bridgford 22 A5
East Calder 40 G3
Eastchurch 11 B11
East Cowes 9 H10
East Cowton 32 D4
East Dean 10 K6
Easter Skeld 57 H4
Eastfield 33 F12
East Grinstead 10 F4
East Harling 24 G4
East Horsley 10 D1
East Ilsley 15 H14
East Kilbride 39 E11
East Leake 22 C4
Eastleigh 9 F9
East Linton 41 F8
East Looe 3 F10
East Markham 28 G6
Eastney 14 C6
East Norton 22 E6
East Oakley 9 C10
Easton
  Dorset 5 F10
  Northants 23 E9
Easton-in-Gordano . .14 J4
Eastry 11 D14
East Wemyss 40 D6
East Wittering 9 H13
East Witton 32 F3
Eastwood 28 K3
East Woodhay 9 A9
Eaton 22 C6
Eaton Socon 23 K10
Ebberston 33 F11
Ebbw Vale 7 A10
Ecclaw 41 G10
Ecclefechan 35 F12
Eccleshall 21 D9
Eccleston 26 A5
Echt 50 G6
Eckington
  Derbys 28 G3
  Worcs 15 B8
Edderton 53 K9
Edenbridge 10 E5
Edgmond 21 E8
Edinburgh 40 F5
Edington 8 B4
Edmundbyers 37 J9

Edwinstowe 28 H5
Edzell 51 L5
Egham 16 J5
Eglwyswrw 12 C5
Egremont 30 C6
Egton 33 D10
Eilean Iarmain 47 K7
Eisgean 55 F5
Elan Village 19 P9
Elgin 49 B13
Elgol 47 K5
Elham 11 E12
Elie 40 C7
Elishaw 36 D7
Elland 27 C12
Ellesmere 20 C5
Ellesmere Port 26 H4
Ellington 37 D11
Ellon 50 D8
Elmswell 25 J4
Elphin 52 G4
Elsdon 37 D8
Elsenham 17 C10
Elstead 9 C14
Elston 22 A6
Elvanfoot 35 B10
Elveden 24 H3
Elvington 33 K8
Elworth 27 J8
Ely 23 G14
Embleton 37 A11
Embo 53 J10
Empingham 23 E8
Emsworth 9 G12
Enderby 22 F4
Endon 21 A10
Enfield 17 F8
Enstone 15 D12
Enterkinfoot 35 C9
Epping 17 E9
Epsom 10 D3
Epworth 28 D6
Eriboll 52 C6
Errogie 48 F6
Errol 45 G14
Erskine 39 C9
Erskine Bridge 39 C9
Escrick 33 K8
Esher 10 C2
Esh Winning 37 J10
Eskdalemuir 35 D13
Eston 32 B7
Etchingham 11 G8
Eton 16 H4
Ettington 15 B11
Etwall 21 C13
Euxton 26 C6
Evanton 48 B7
Evercreech 8 D1
Everleigh 8 B7
Evershot 5 C9
Evesham 15 B9
Ewell 10 C3
Ewhurst 10 F1
Ewyas Harold 14 D2
Exbourne 3 A14
Exeter 4 D3
Exford 6 H7
Exminster 4 E3
Exmouth 4 F3
Exton 23 D8
Eyam 27 H13
Eye
  Pboro 23 E11
  Suff 25 H6
Eyemouth 41 G12
Eyethorne 11 E13
Eynsford 10 C6
Eynsham 15 F13

F

Faddiley 20 A6
Fairbourne 19 J6
Fairford 15 F10
Fairlie 38 E7
Fairlight 11 H9
Fakenham 24 B4

Fala 40 G7
Faldingworth 29 F9
Falkirk 39 B13
Falkland 40 C5
Falmer 10 J4
Falmouth 2 H6
Falstone 36 E6
Fareham 9 G10
Faringdon 15 G11
Farnborough
Hants 9 B13
W Berks 15 H13
Farndon 20 A5
Farnham 9 C13
Farnworth 27 E8
Farr 48 E7
Fasag 46 F9
Faslane 38 A7
Fauldhouse 40 G2
Faversham 11 C11
Fawley 9 G9
Fazeley 21 F13
Fearn 49 A9
Fearnan 45 E9
Feckenham 21 K11
Felixstowe 25 M8
Felton 37 C10
Feltwell 24 F2
Fenny Bentley 21 A12
Fenny Compton 15 A13
Fenny Stratford 16 B3
Fenwick 39 F9
Feock 2 H6
Feolin Ferry 43 M6
Ferndown 8 H5
Ferness 49 D10
Fernhurst 9 E14
Ferryhill 32 A4
Ferryside 12 F7
Fettercairn 51 K5
Filby 24 D9
Filey 33 F13
Fillongley 21 H13
Filton 14 J5
Fincham 24 E1
Finchingfield 17 B11
Finchley 16 F7
Findhorn 49 B11
Findochty 50 A3
Findon 10 J2
Finedon 23 H8
Finningley 28 E5
Finstown 56 E3
Fintry 39 B11
Fionnphort 42 F4
Fishbourne 9 H10
Fishguard 12 C3
Fishnish 42 D8
Fishtoft 23 A12
Flamborough 33 G14
Fleet 9 B13
Fleetwood 31 K9
Flimby 35 K11
Flint 26 H3
Flitwick 16 B5
Flodden 41 K12
Flookburgh 31 G9
Fochabers 50 B2
Foel 19 J10
Folkestone 11 F13
Folkingham 23 B9
Fontmell Magna 8 F3
Ford 43 H10
Forden 20 F3
Fordham 25 H1
Fordingbridge 8 F6
Fordyce 50 A4
Forest Row 10 F5
Forfar 51 M3
Formby 26 E3
Forres 49 C11
Forsinain 53 D11
Forsinard 53 D10
Fort Augustus 48 H4
Fort George
Highland 49 C8
Jersey 4 Jersey
Forth 40 H2
Forth Road Bridge 40 E4
Fortrie 50 C5
Fortrose 49 C8
Fortuneswell 5 F10
Fort William 44 B3
Fothergill 35 K11
Fotheringhay 23 F9
Foulden 41 H12
Foulsham 24 C5
Fountainhall 40 J7
Four Lanes 2 H4
Fovant 8 E5
Fowey 3 F9
Fownhope 14 C4
Foxdale 30 H2
Foyers 48 F6
Fraddon 2 F6
Framlingham 25 J7
Frampton on Severn 14 F6
Frant 10 F6
Fraserburgh 50 A8
Freckleton 26 C5
Freethorpe 24 E9
Fremington 6 H4
Frensham 9 C13
Freshwater 9 J8
Freshwater East 12 G4
Fressingfield 24 H7
Freswick 53 B15
Freuchie 40 C5
Friday Bridge 23 E13
Fridaythorpe 33 H10
Frimley 9 B13
Frinton-on-Sea 25 P7
Friockheim 51 M4
Frizington 30 C6
Frodsham 26 H6
Frome 8 C2
Frongoch 18 G9
Froxfield 15 K11
Fulbourn 23 K14
Fulford 33 K8
Fulwood 26 B6
Funzie 57 C7
Furnace 44 J2
Fyfield 17 E10
Fyvie 50 D6

G

Gaerwen 18 C4
Gaick Lodge 49 K8
Gailey 21 E10
Gainford 32 C3
Gainsborough 28 F7
Gairloch 46 D8
Gairlochy 44 A3
Galashiels 40 K7
Galgate 31 J10
Galmisdale 47 N4
Galmpton 4 H2
Galston 39 G10
Gamlingay 23 K11
Garbhallt 38 A5
Garboldisham 24 G5
Gardenstown 50 A7
Garelochhead 38 A7
Garforth 28 A3
Gargrave 32 J1
Gargunnock 39 A12
Garlieston 34 J5
Garmouth 50 A2
Garrow 45 E10
Garsdale Head 31 E13
Garstang 31 K10
Garston 26 G4
Garton-on-the-Wolds 33 H11
Garvald 41 F8
Garvard 43 J5
Garve 48 B4
Gatehouse of Fleet 34 H6
Gateshead 37 G11
Gatley 27 G9
Gatwick Airport 10 E3
Gawthwaite 31 F8
Gaydon 15 A12
Gayton 24 D2
Gaywood 24 C1
Gearraidh na h-Aibhne 55 D4
Geary 46 E2
Geddington 22 G7
Gedney 23 C13
Gedney Drove End 23 C13
Georgeham 6 H3
Gerrards Cross 16 G5
Gifford 41 G8
Giggleswick 31 H14
Gillingham
Dorset 5 A11
Medway 17 J12
Gilmerton 45 G10
Gilsland 36 G5
Gilwern 14 E1
Giosla 55 E3
Girton 23 J13
Girvan 34 D3
Gisburn 31 K14
Gladestry 14 A1
Glamis 51 N2
Glanaman 13 E10
Glanton 37 B9
Glasbury 13 C15
Glasgow 39 D10
Glasserton 34 K5
Glasson 31 J10
Glastonbury 7 H14
Glemsford 25 L3
Glenbarr 38 G1
Glenborrodale 42 B8
Glenbrittle 47 J4
Glencaple 35 G10
Glencarse 45 G14
Glencoe 44 D3
Glendoll Lodge 51 K1
Gleneagles 45 H11
Glenelg 47 K8
Glenfinnan 47 N9
Glenluce 34 H3
Glenmaye 30 G2
Glenmore Lodge 49 H10
Glenprosen Lodge 51 L1
Glenrothes 40 C5
Glenstriven 38 C5
Glentrool Village 34 F4
Glenwhilly 34 F3
Glinton 23 E10
Glossop 27 F11
Gloucester 14 E7
Glusburn 27 A11
Glutt Lodge 53 E11
Glyn Ceiriog 20 C3
Glyncorrwg 13 G12
Glynde 10 J5
Glyndyfrdwy 20 B2
Glyn Neath 13 F12
Gnosall 21 D9
Goathland 33 D10
Gobowen 20 C4
Godalming 9 C14
Godmanchester 23 H11
Godshill 9 J10
Godstone 10 E4
Goldhanger 25 Q4
Golspie 53 J10
Goodrich 14 E4
Goodwick 12 C3
Goole 28 B6
Goonhavern 2 F5
Gordon 41 J9
Gorebridge 40 G6
Gorey 5 Jersey
Goring 16 G1
Goring-by-Sea 10 J2
Gorleston-on-Sea 24 E10
Gorran Haven 3 H8
Gorseinon 13 G9
Gorslas 13 E9
Gosberton 23 B11
Gosfield 25 N2
Gosforth 30 D6
Gosport 9 H11
Goswick 41 J13
Gotham 22 C4
Goudhurst 11 F8
Gourdon 51 K7
Gourock 38 C7
Gowerton 13 G9
Grabhair 55 F5
Grain 11 B9
Grainthorpe 29 E12
Grampound 2 G7
Gramsdal 54 D5
Grangemouth 40 E2
Grange-over-Sands 31 G10
Grantham 23 B8
Grantown-on-Spey 49 F11
Grantshouse 41 G11
Grasby 29 D9
Grasmere 31 D9
Grassington 32 H2
Grateley 8 C7
Gravesend 17 H11
Grayrigg 31 E11
Grays 17 H11
Grayshott 9 D13
Great Ayton 32 C7
Great Baddow 17 E12
Great Barford 23 K10
Great Bentley 25 N6
Great Bridgeford 21 D9
Great Broughton 32 D7
Great Chesterford 17 A10
Great Clifton 30 B6
Great Dunmow 17 C11
Great Ellingham 24 F5
Great Gidding 23 G10
Greatham 32 B6
Great Harwood 27 B8
Great Horwood 16 B2
Great Malvern 14 B6
Great Massingham 24 C2
Great Missenden 16 E4
Great Oakley 25 N7
Great Sampford 17 B11
Great Shefford 15 J12
Great Shelford 23 K13
Great Somerford 15 H8
Great Staunton 23 H10
Great Torrington 6 K3
Great Wakering 17 G14
Great Waltham 17 D12
Great Witley 21 K8
Great Yarmouth 24 E10
Green Hammerton 32 J6
Greenhead 36 G5
Greenholm 39 G10
Greenlaw 41 J10
Greenloaning 45 J10
Greenock 38 C7
Greenodd 31 F9
Greenway 12 D4
Greenwich 10 B4
Gretna 36 G2
Gretna Green 36 G2
Gretton 23 F8
Greystoke 31 A10
Grimsby 29 D11
Gritley 56 F5
Grizebeck 31 F8
Groby 22 E4
Grove 15 G13
Grundisburgh 25 L7
Gualachulain 44 E3
Guard Bridge 40 B7
Guestling Green 11 H9
Guildford 10 E1
Guildtown 45 F13
Guilsfield 20 E3
Guisborough 33 C8
Guiseley 27 A12
Gullane 40 E7
Gunnerside 32 E1
Gunnislake 3 D12
Gunnista 57 H6
Gutcher 57 B6
Gwalchmai 18 C3
Gwaun-Cae-Gurwen 13 E10
Gwbert 12 B5
Gweek 2 J4
Gwennap 2 H5
Gwyddelwern 18 F10
Gwytherin 18 D8
Gyre 56 F3

H

Hackney 10 A4
Hackthorpe 31 B11
Haddenham
Bucks 16 E2
Cambs 23 H13
Haddington 41 F8
Haddiscoe 24 F9
Hadleigh
Essex 17 G13
Suff. 25 L5
Hadlow 10 E7
Hadnall 20 D6
Hagworthingham 29 H12
Hailsham 10 J6
Hainton 29 F10
Halberton 4 B4
Halesowen 21 H10
Halesworth 24 H8
Halford 15 B11
Halifax 27 C11
Halkirk 53 C13
Halland 10 H6
Hallow 14 A7
Hallworthy 3 C9
Halstead 25 M3
Halton 31 H11
Haltwhistle 36 G6
Halwill Junction 3 B12
Hambledon 9 F11
Hamble-le-Rice 9 G9
Hambleton
Lancs 26 A4
N Yorks 28 A4
Hamerton 23 H10
Hamilton 39 E12
Hammersmith & Fulham 10 B3
Hamnavoe
Shetland 57 E6
Shetland 57 J4
Hampstead Norreys 15 J14
Hampton in Arden 21 H13
Hamstreet 11 F11
Handcross 10 G3
Hannington 9 B10
Harbury 22 J2
Harby 22 B6
Hardingstone 22 K6
Harewood 27 A14
Haringey 10 A4
Harlech 18 G5
Harleston 24 G7
Harlow 17 E9
Haroldswick 57 A7
Harpenden 16 D6
Harrietfield 45 F11
Harrietsham 11 D9
Harrington 30 B5
Harris 47 M3
Harrogate 32 J4
Harrold 23 K8
Harrow 16 G6
Harston 23 K13
Hartburn 37 E9
Hartest 25 K3
Hartfield 10 F5
Harthill 40 G2
Hartington 27 J12
Hartland 6 J1
Hartlebury 21 J9
Hartlepool 32 A7
Hartley
Kent 17 J11
Northumb. 37 F12
Hartley Wintney 9 B12
Hartpury 14 D6
Hartshill 22 F2
Harvington 15 B9
Harwell 15 H13
Harwich 25 M7
Harworth 28 E5
Haselbury Plucknett 5 C8

Haslemere 9 D13
Haslingden 27 C8
Hassocks 10 H4
Hastigrow 53 C14
Hastings 11 J9
Haswell 37 J12
Hatch Beauchamp . . . 4 B7
Hatfield
  Herts 16 E7
  S Yorks 28 D5
Hatfield Heath 17 D10
Hatfield Peverel . . . 17 D13
Hatherleigh 3 A13
Hathersage 27 G13
Hatton
  Aberds 50 D9
  Derbys 21 C13
Haughley 25 J5
Haugh of Urr 35 G8
Haughton 21 D9
Havant 9 G12
Haverfordwest 12 E3
Haverhill 17 A11
Haverigg 30 F7
Havering 17 G10
Hawarden 26 J4
Hawes 31 E14
Hawick 36 B4
Hawkchurch 4 D7
Hawkesbury Upton . . 14 H6
Hawkhurst 11 G8
Hawkinge 11 F13
Hawkshead 31 E9
Hawnby 32 E7
Haworth 27 B11
Hawsker 33 D11
Haxby 33 J8
Haxey 28 D6
Haydon Bridge 36 G7
Hayfield 27 G11
Hayle 2 H3
Hay-on-Wye 14 B1
Hayton
  Cumb 36 H4
  E Yorks 33 K10
Haywards Heath . . . 10 G4
Hazel Grove 27 G10
Hazlemere 16 F4
Heacham 24 B1
Headcorn 11 E9
Headley 9 D13
Heanor 22 A3
Heath End 9 A10
Heathfield 10 H6
Heathrow Airport . . 16 H5
Hebburn 37 G12
Hebden Bridge 27 C10
Heckington 23 A10
Hedge End 9 F10
Hednesford 21 E11
Hedon 29 B10
Heighington 32 B4
Heilam 52 B6
Helensburgh 39 B8
Hellifield 31 J14
Helmsdale 53 G12
Helmsley 33 F8
Helperby 32 G6
Helpringham 23 A10
Helsby 26 H5
Helston 2 J4
Hemel Hempstead . . 16 E5
Hemingbrough 28 A5
Hempnall 24 F7
Hempton 24 C4
Hemsby 24 D9
Hemsworth 28 C3
Hemyock 4 B5
Henfield 10 H3
Hengoed 7 B10
Henley-in-Arden . . . 21 K12
Henley-on-Thames . . 16 G2
Henllan 18 D10
Henlow 16 B6
Henstridge 5 B11
Herbrandston 12 F2

Hereford 14 C4
Heriot 40 H7
Hermitage 15 J14
Herne Bay 11 C12
Herstmonceux 10 H7
Herston 56 G4
Hertford 17 D8
Hessle 29 B9
Heswall 26 G3
Hethersett 24 E6
Hetton-le-Hole 37 J12
Hexham 37 G8
Heybridge 17 E13
Heysham 31 H10
Heytesbury 8 C4
Heywood 27 D9
Hibaldstow 29 D8
Higham 17 H12
Higham Ferrers 23 J8
High Bentham 31 G12
High Bickington 6 K4
Highbridge 7 G12
Highclere 9 B9
High Ercall 20 E7
High Hesket 36 J3
High Legh 27 G8
Highley 21 H8
Hightae 35 F11
Highworth 15 G11
High Wycombe 16 F3
Hilborough 24 E3
Hildenborough 10 E6
Hilgay 24 F1
Hillingdon 16 G5
Hillington 24 C2
Hillswick 57 E3
Hilmarton 15 J9
Hilton 21 C13
Hinckley 22 F3
Hinderwell 33 C10
Hindhead 9 D13
Hindley 26 E7
Hindon 8 D4
Hingham 24 E5
Hinstock 20 D8
Hirwaun 13 F13
Histon 23 J13
Hitchin 16 B6
Hockley 17 F13
Hockliffe 16 C4
Hoddesdon 17 E8
Hodnet 20 D7
Hoff 31 C12
Holbeach 23 C12
Holbeach Drove . . . 23 D12
Holbrook 25 M6
Holford 7 G10
Holkham 24 A3
Holland-on-Sea 25 P7
Hollandstoun 56 A7
Hollym 29 B12
Holme-on-Spalding-moor 28 A7
Holmer 14 B4
Holmes Chapel 27 J8
Holmfirth 27 E12
Holsworthy 3 A11
Holt
  Norf 24 B5
  Wrex 20 A5
Holyhead 18 B2
Holywell 26 H2
Honington 23 A8
Honiton 4 D5
Hook 9 B12
Hook Norton 15 C12
Hope 26 K4
Hopeman 49 A12
Hope under
  Dinmore 14 A4
Horam 10 H6
Horden 37 J13
Horley 10 E3
Horncastle 29 H11
Horndean 9 F12
Horningsham 8 C3
Hornsea 33 K13
Horrabridge 3 E13
Horringer 25 J3

Horsey 24 C9
Horsford 24 D6
Horsforth 27 B13
Horsham 10 F2
Horsham St Faith . . 24 D7
Horsted Keynes 10 G4
Horton
  Northants 22 K7
  Som 4 B7
Horton in
  Ribblesdale 31 G14
Horwich 26 D7
Houghton-le-
  Spring 37 H12
Houghton Regis . . . 16 C5
Hounslow 10 B2
Hove 10 J3
Hoveton 24 D7
Hovingham 33 G8
Howden 28 B6
Howpasley 36 C2
Hoxne 24 H6
Hoylake 26 G3
Hucknall 28 K4
Huddersfield 27 D12
Hugh Town 2 C3
Hulland Ward 21 B13
Hullavington 14 H7
Hullbridge 17 F13
Hulme End 27 K12
Humber Bridge . . . 29 B9
Humberston 29 D11
Humshaugh 37 F8
Hundred House . . . 13 A15
Hungerford 15 K12
Hunmanby 33 G12
Hunstanton 24 A1
Huntford 36 C5
Huntingdon 23 H11
Huntley 14 E6
Huntly 50 C4
Hurlford 39 G9
Hurliness 56 H2
Hurn 8 H6
Hursley 9 E9
Hurstbourne Tarrant . 9 B8
Hurstpierpoint 10 H3
Hurworth-on-Tees . . 32 C5
Husbands Bosworth . 22 G5
Husinish 55 F2
Huttoft 29 G14
Hutton 26 C5
Hutton Cranswick . . 33 J12
Hutton-le-Hole 33 E9
Hutton Rudby 32 D6
Huyton 26 F5
Hyde 27 F10
Hynish 42 E1
Hythe
  Hants 9 G9
  Kent 11 F12

I

Ibsey 8 G6
Ibstock 22 D2
Icklingham 25 H2
Idmiston 8 D7
Ilchester 5 A9
Ilderton 37 A9
Ilfracombe 6 H2
Ilkeston 22 A3
Ilkley 32 K3
Illogan 2 G4
Ilminster 4 B7
Immingham 29 C10
Inchnadamph 52 F4
Inchture 45 F14
Ingatestone 17 F11
Ingleton 31 G12
Ingoldmells 29 H14
Ingram 37 B9
Ingrave 17 F11
Inkberrow 15 A9
Innellan 38 C6
Innerleithen 40 K6
Innermessan 34 G2
Insch 50 E5

Instow 6 J3
Inver 53 K10
Inverallochy 50 A9
Inveran 52 J7
Inveraray 44 J2
Inverarity 51 N3
Inverbervie 51 K7
Invergarry 48 H4
Invergordon 49 B8
Invergowrie 51 P2
Inverie 47 L7
Inverinate 47 J9
Inverkeilor 51 M5
Inverkeithing 40 E4
Inverkirkaig 52 F2
Inverlochlarig 44 H6
Invermoriston 48 G5
Inverness 48 D7
Inversnaid 44 J5
Inverurie 50 E6
Ipswich 25 L6
Irchester 23 J8
Irlam 27 F8
Ironbridge 20 F7
Irthlingborough . . . 23 H8
Irvine 39 G8
Isbister 57 C4
Isleham 25 H1
Isle of Whithorn . . . 34 K5
Islington 10 A4
Islip 15 E14
Ivinghoe 16 D4
Ivybridge 3 F14
Iwerne Minster 8 F3
Ixworth 25 H4

J

Jamestown 39 B8
Jarrow 37 G12
Jaywick 25 P6
Jedburgh 36 A5
John o' Groats 53 A15
Johnshaven 51 L7
Johnston 12 F3
Johnstone 39 D9

K

Kames 38 C4
Kea 2 G5
Kearvaig 52 A4
Kedington 17 A11
Keelby 29 C10
Keele 21 B9
Kegworth 22 C3
Keighley 27 A11
Keillmore 38 B1
Keiss 53 B15
Keith 50 B3
Keld 31 D14
Kellas 49 C12
Kelsale 25 J8
Kelsall 26 J6
Kelso 41 K10
Keltneyburn 45 E9
Kelty 40 D4
Kelvedon 17 D13
Kelynack 2 J1
Kemble 15 G9
Kemnay 50 F6
Kempsey 14 B7
Kempston 16 A5
Kemsing 10 D6
Kendal 31 E11
Kenilworth 22 H1
Kenmore 45 E9
Kennacraig 38 D3
Kennethmont 50 E4
Kennford 4 E3
Kenninghall 24 G5
Kennington 15 F14
Kensington &
  Chelsea 10 B3
Kentford 25 J2
Kentisbeare 4 C4
Kerry 20 H2

Kerrysdale 46 D8
Kershopefoot 36 E3
Kesgrave 25 L7
Kessingland 24 G10
Keswick 31 B8
Kettering 22 H7
Kettletoft 56 C6
Kettlewell 32 G1
Ketton 23 E8
Kew Bridge 10 B3
Kexby 28 F7
Keyingham 29 B11
Keymer 10 H4
Keynsham 14 K5
Keysoe 23 J9
Keyworth 22 B5
Kibworth
  Beauchamp 22 F5
Kidderminster 21 H9
Kidlington 15 E14
Kidsgrove 21 A9
Kidstones 32 F1
Kidwelly 12 F8
Kielder 36 D5
Kilberry 38 D2
Kilbirnie 39 E8
Kilcadzow 39 F13
Kilchattan 38 E6
Kilchenzie 38 H1
Kilchiaran 43 M4
Kilchoan 42 B6
Kilchrenan 44 G2
Kilcreggan 38 B7
Kildonan 53 F11
Kilfinan 38 C4
Kilham 33 H12
Kilkhampton 3 A10
Killamarsh 28 F3
Killean 38 F1
Killearn 39 B10
Killin 44 F7
Killinghall 32 J4
Kilmacolm 39 D8
Kilmaluag 46 D4
Kilmany 40 A6
Kilmarnock 39 G9
Kilmartin 38 A3
Kilmaurs 39 F9
Kilmelford 42 G10
Kilmore 42 F10
Kilmory
  Argyll 38 C2
  Highland 42 A7
  Highland 47 L3
Kilmuir 49 A8
Kilninver 42 F10
Kilnsea 29 C13
Kilrenny 41 C8
Kilsby 22 H4
Kilsyth 39 C12
Kilwinning 38 F7
Kimbolton 23 J9
Kimpton 16 D6
Kinbrace 53 F10
Kinbuck 45 J10
Kincardine
  Fife 40 E2
  Highland 52 K8
Kincardine Bridge . . 40 E2
Kincraig 49 H9
Kineton 15 A12
Kingarth 38 E5
Kinghorn 40 E5
Kingsbarns 41 B8
Kingsbridge 4 J1
Kingsbury 21 G13
Kingsclere 9 B10
King's Cliffe 23 F9
Kingsdown 11 E14
Kingskerswell 4 G2
Kingsland 20 K5
Kings Langley 16 E5
Kingsley
  Hants 9 D12
  Staffs 21 B11
King's Lynn 24 D1
King's Somborne . . . 9 D8
King's Sutton 15 C14
Kingsteignton 4 F2

King's Thorn 14 C4
Kingston
  Devon 3 G14
  London 10 C2
Kingston Bagpuize .15 G13
Kingston upon Hull . . 29 B9
Kingswear 4 J2
Kingswood 14 J5
King's Worthy 9 D10
Kington 14 A2
Kingussie 49 H8
Kinloch
  Highland 47 M4
  Highland 52 E5
Kinlochbervie 52 C4
Kinlocheil 47 N9
Kinlochewe 46 E10
Kinlochleven 44 C3
Kinlochmoidart 42 A9
Kinloch Rannoch 45 D8
Kinloss 49 B11
Kinmel Bay 18 C9
Kinross 40 C4
Kintessack 49 C10
Kintore 50 F6
Kinuachdrachd 43 J9
Kinver 21 H9
Kippax 28 A3
Kippen 39 A11
Kirkabister 57 J5
Kirkbampton 35 H10
Kirkbean 35 H13
Kirkbride 35 H13
Kirkburton 27 D12
Kirkby 26 F5
Kirkby-in-Ashfield . . 28 J4
Kirkby-in-Furness . .31 F8
Kirkby Lonsdale . . .31 G12
Kirkby Malzeard . . .32 G4
Kirkbymoorside 33 F8
Kirkby Stephen 31 D13
Kirkby Thore 31 B12
Kirkcaldy 40 D5
Kirkcolm 34 G1
Kirkconnel 35 B8
Kirkcowan 34 G4
Kirkcudbright 34 H8
Kirkham 26 B5
Kirkinner 34 H5
Kirkintilloch 39 C11
Kirkland 35 D9
Kirkliston 40 F4
Kirkmichael
  Perth 45 C12
  S Ayrs 34 C4
Kirk Michael 30 F3
Kirknewton 41 K12
Kirkoswald
  Cumb 36 J4
  S Ayrs 34 C3
Kirkpatrick Durham . 35 F8
Kirkpatrick Fleming 35 F13
Kirkton of Glenisla .45 C14
Kirkton of Largo . . .40 C7
Kirkwall 56 E4
Kirkwhelpington . . .37 E9
Kirriemuir 51 M2
Kirtling 25 K1
Kirtlington 15 D14
Kirton 23 B11
Kirton in Lindsey . . 29 E8
Knaresborough 32 J5
Knayton 32 F6
Knebworth 16 D7
Knighton 20 J3
Knott End-on-Sea. . .31 K9
Knottingley 28 B3
Knowle 21 J12
Knutsford 27 H8
Kyleakin 47 J7
Kyle of Lochalsh . . .47 J7
Kylerhea 47 J7
Kylestrome 52 E4

Laceby 29 D11
Lacock 15 K8
Ladock 2 G6
Ladybank 40 B6
Lagg
  Argyll 43 L7
  N Ayrs 38 H4
Laggan
  Highland 48 J4
  Highland 48 J7
  Moray 50 D2
Laide 46 B9
Lairg 52 H7
Lakenheath 24 G2
Lamberhurst 10 F7
Lambeth 10 B4
Lambley 36 H5
Lambourn 15 J12
Lamlash 38 G5
Lampeter 13 B9
Lanark 39 F13
Lancaster 31 H10
Lanchester 37 J10
Lancing 10 J2
Landkey 6 J4
Landrake 3 F11
Langford Budville . .7 J10
Langham 22 D7
Langholm 36 E2
Langport 7 J13
Langsett 27 E13
Langtoft
  E Yorks 33 H12
  Lincs 23 D10
Langton Matravers . .8 K4
Langtree 6 K3
Langwathby 31 A11
Langwell 52 H8
Lanivet 3 E8
Lapford 4 C1
Larbert 39 B13
Largs 38 E7
Larkhall 39 E12
Larkhill 8 C6
Lasswade 40 G6
Latchingdon 17 E13
Latheron 53 E14
Lauder 41 J8
Laugharne 12 E6
Launceston 3 C11
Laurencekirk 51 K6
Laurieston 34 G7
Lavendon 23 K8
Lavenham 25 L4
Lawers 45 F8
Laxey 30 G4
Laxfield 25 H7
Laxford Bridge 52 D4
Laxton 28 H6
Layer de la Haye . . .25 P4
Lazonby 36 J4
Lea 28 F7
Leadburn 40 H5
Leadenham 29 J8
Leaden Roding 17 D11
Leadgate 37 H10
Leadhills 35 B9
Leasingham 29 K9
Leatherhead 10 D2
Lechlade-on-
  Thames 15 G11
Ledbury 14 C6
Ledmore 52 G4
Leeds 27 B13
Leedstown 2 H3
Leek 27 K10
Leeming Bar 32 E4
Lee-on-the-Solent . .9 H10
Legbourne 29 F12
Leicester 22 E4
Leigh
  Grt Manchester 26 E7
  Worcs 14 A6
Leighton Buzzard . .16 C4
Leintwardine 20 J5
Leiston 25 J9

Leith 40 F5
Leitholm 41 J10
Lelant 2 H3
Lendalfoot 34 D2
Lenham 11 D10
Lennoxtown 39 C11
Leominster 14 A3
Lephin 46 G1
Le Planel . . . . 4 Guern
Lerwick 57 H5
Lesbury 37 B11
Leslie 40 C5
Lesmahagow 39 F13
Leswalt 34 G1
Letchworth 16 B7
Lettan 56 B7
Letterston 12 D3
Lettoch 49 E12
Leuchars 40 A7
Leumrabhagh 55 F5
Leven
  E Yorks 33 K13
  Fife 40 C6
Leverburgh / An t-
  Ob 55 J2
Lewes 10 J5
Lewisham 10 B4
Lewiston 48 F6
Leyburn 32 E3
Leyland 26 C6
Leysdown-on-Sea. .11 C11
Lhanbryde 49 B13
Liatrie 48 E3
Lichfield 21 F12
Lidgate 25 K2
Lifton 3 C11
Lilleshall 21 E8
Lilliesleaf 36 C2
Lincoln 29 G8
Lindale 31 F10
Lingfield 10 E4
Linkinhorne 3 D11
Linksness 56 F2
Linlithgow 40 F2
Linslade 16 C4
Linton 17 A10
Liphook 9 E13
Liskeard 3 E10
Liss 9 E12
Lissett 33 J13
Litcham 24 D3
Litherland 26 F4
Littleborough 27 D10
Littlehampton 10 J1
Littlemill 49 C10
Littleport 23 G14
Little Shelford 23 K13
Littlestone-on-Sea 11 G11
Little Stukeley 23 H11
Little Walsingham . .24 B4
Liverpool 26 G4
Liverpool Airport . .26 G5
Livingston 40 G3
Lizard 2 K4
Llanaber 19 J5
Llanaelhaiarn 18 F3
Llanafan-fawr 19 Q9
Llanarmon 26 K2
Llanarmon Dyffryn
  Ceiriog 20 C2
Llanarth 19 Q4
Llanbadarn Fynydd . 20 J2
Llanbedr 18 H5
Llanbedrog 18 G3
Llanberis 18 E5
Llanbister 20 J2
Llanbrynmair 19 K9
Llanddewi-Brefi . . .19 Q6
Llanddulas 18 C8
Llandeilo 13 D10
Llandinam 19 M10
Llandissilio 12 D5
Llandogo 14 F4
Llandovery 13 C15
Llandrillo 18 G10
Llandrindod Wells .19 P10
Llandudno 18 B7
Llandybie 13 E10
Llandyfriog 12 B7

Llandygwydd 12 B6
Llandyrnog 26 J2
Llandysul 12 B8
Llanelidan 20 B1
Llanelli 13 F9
Llanelltyd 19 J7
Llanenddwyn 18 H5
Llanerchymedd 18 B4
Llanfyrfyl 19 K10
Llanfaethlu 18 B3
Llanfair Caereinion . 20 F2
Llanfairfechan 18 C6
Llanfairpwllgwngyll .18 C5
Llanfair Talhaiarn . .18 C9
Llanfechain 20 E2
Llanfechell 18 B3
Llan Ffestiniog 18 F7
Llanfihangel-ar-arth 13 C8
Llanfrynach 13 D14
Llanfyllin 20 E2
Llangadfan 19 J10
Llangadog 13 D11
Llangammarch
  Wells 13 B13
Llangefni 18 C4
Llangeitho 19 Q6
Llangelynin 19 K5
Llangennech 13 F9
Llangernyw 18 D8
Llanglydwen 12 D5
Llangoed 18 C6
Llangollen 20 B3
Llangorse 13 D15
Llangranog 12 A7
Llangunllo 20 J3
Llangurig 19 N9
Llangwm 14 F3
Llangybi 19 Q6
Llangynidr 13 E15
Llangynog 18 H10
Llanharan 7 C9
Llanidloes 19 M9
Llanilar 19 N6
Llanllyfni 18 E4
Llannor 18 G3
Llanon 19 P5
Llanpumsaint 12 D8
Llanrhaeadr-ym-
  Mochnant 20 D2
Llanrhian 12 C2
Llanrhidian 13 G8
Llanrhystyd 19 N5
Llanrug 18 D5
Llanrwst 18 D7
Llansannan 18 D9
Llansawel 13 C10
Llanstephan 12 E7
Llanthony 14 D1
Llantrisant 7 C9
Llantwit-Major 13 K13
Llanuwchllyn 18 G8
Llanvihangel
  Crucorney 14 D2
Llanwddyn 19 J10
Llanwenog 13 B8
Llanwrda 13 C11
Llanwrtyd Wells . . .13 B12
LlanybIodwel 20 D3
Llanybydder 13 B9
Llanymynech 20 D3
Llanystumdwy 18 G4
Llay 20 A4
Lledrod 19 N6
Llithfaen 18 F3
Llwyngwril 19 J6
Llyswen 13 C15
Loanhead 40 G5
Lochailort 47 N7
Lochaline 42 D8
Lochans 34 H1
Locharbriggs 35 E10
Loch Baghasdail /
  Lochboisdale 54 H4
Lochboisdale / Loch
  Baghasdail 54 H4
Lochbuie 42 F8
Lochcarron 46 G9
Loch Choire Lodge . 52 E8
Lochdon 42 E9

Lochearnhead 44 G7
Loch Euphoirt 54 C5
Lochgair 38 A4
Lochgelly 40 D4
Lochgilphead 38 B3
Lochgoilhead 44 J4
Lochinver 52 F2
Lochmaben 35 E11
Lochmaddy / Loch nam
  Madadh 54 C6
Loch nam Madadh /
  Lochmaddy 54 C6
Lochranza 38 E4
Loch Sgioport 54 F5
Lochwinnoch 39 D8
Lockerbie 35 E12
Lockton 33 E10
Loddiswell 4 J1
Loddon 24 F8
Loftus 33 C9
Logan 34 A7
London 10 B4
London Colney 16 E6
Long Ashton 14 K4
Long Bennington . . .22 A7
Longbenton 37 G11
Longbridge Deverill . 8 C3
Long Clawson 22 C6
Long Compton 15 C11
Long Crendon 16 E1
Longdon 14 C7
Long Eaton 22 B3
Longford 14 D7
Longforgan 51 P2
Longformacus 41 H10
Longframlington . . .37 C10
Longhope 56 G3
Longhorsley 37 D10
Longhoughton 37 B11
Long Itchington . . .22 J3
Long Melford 25 L3
Longnor 27 J11
Long Preston 31 J14
Longridge 26 B7
Longside 50 C9
Long Stratton 24 F6
Long Sutton 23 C13
Longtown
  Cumb 36 G2
  Hereford 14 D2
Loose 11 D8
Lossiemouth 49 A13
Lostock Gralam . . .26 H8
Lostwithiel 3 F8
Loth 56 C6
Loughborough 22 C4
Loughor 13 G9
Loughton 17 F9
Louth 29 F12
Lowdham 22 A5
Lower Beeding 10 G3
Lower Killeyan 43 P4
Lower Langford 7 F13
Lower Mayland 17 E14
Lower Shiplake 16 H2
Lowestoft 24 F10
Lowick 41 J13
Loxhore 6 J13
Loxwood 10 F1
Lubcroy 52 H5
Lucker 41 K14
Ludborough 29 E11
Ludford 29 F10
Ludgershall 8 B7
Ludgvan 2 H2
Ludham 24 D8
Ludlow 20 J6
Lugton 39 E9
Lugwardine 14 B4
Lumphanan 50 G4
Lumsden 50 E3
Luss 39 A8
Lusta 46 F2
Luston 16 C5
Lutterworth 22 G4
Lutton 23 G10
Lybster 53 E14

Lydd 11 H11
Lydd on Sea 11 H11
Lydford 3 C13
Lydham 20 G4
Lydney 14 F5
Lyme Regis 4 D7
Lyminge 11 E12
Lymington 9 H8
Lymm 26 G2
Lympne 11 F12
Lympstone 4 E3
Lyndhurst 8 G7
Lyneham 15 J9
Lyness 56 G3
Lynmouth 6 G6
Lynton 6 G6
Lytchett Minster 8 H4
Lytham St Anne's 26 C4
Lythe 33 C10

M

Mablethorpe 29 F13
Macclesfield 27 H10
Macduff 50 A5
Machen 7 C11
Machrihanish 38 H1
Machynlleth 19 K7
Macmerry 40 F7
Madeley 21 B8
Madley 14 C3
Maentwrog 18 G6
Maesteg 13 H12
Maghull 26 E4
Magor 14 H3
Maiden Bradley 8 D3
Maidenhead 16 H3
Maiden Newton 5 D9
Maidstone 11 D8
Maldon 17 E13
Malham 31 H14
Mallaig 47 M6
Mallwyd 19 J8
Malmesbury 15 H8
Malpas 20 B6
Maltby 28 E4
Maltby le Marsh 29 F13
Malton 33 G9
Manafon 20 F2
Manby 29 F13
Manchester 27 F9
Manchester Airport . .27 G9
Manea 23 G13
Mangotsfield 14 J5
Manningtree 25 M6
Manorbier 12 G4
Mansfield 28 H4
Mansfield
  Woodhouse 28 H4
Manton 22 E7
Marazion 2 J3
Marbhig 55 F6
March 23 F13
Marden
  Hereford 14 B4
  Kent 11 E8
Mareham le Fen 29 H11
Maresfield 10 G5
Marfleet 29 B10
Margam 13 H11
Margate 11 C14
Marham 24 D2
Market Bosworth 22 E3
Market Deeping 23 D10
Market Drayton 20 C7
Market Harborough . .22 G6
Market Lavington 8 B5
Market Rasen 29 F10
Market Warsop 28 H4
Market Weighton 33 K10
Markfield 22 D3
Markinch 40 C6
Marks Tey 25 N4
Markyate 16 D5

Marlborough
  Devon 4 K1
  Wilts 15 K10
Marlow 16 G3
Marnhull 5 B11
Marple 27 G10
Marshchapel 29 E12
Marshfield 14 J6
Marske-by-the-Sea . .33 B8
Marston Magna 5 A9
Martham 24 D9
Martin 8 F5
Martley 21 K8
Martock 5 B8
Marton 28 F7
Marykirk 51 L5
Marypark 49 E12
Maryport 35 K11
Mary Tavy 3 D13
Marywell
  Aberds 51 H4
  Angus 51 N5
Masham 32 F4
Mathry 12 C2
Matlock 28 H1
Mattishall 24 D5
Mauchline 39 H9
Maud 50 C8
Maughold 30 F4
Mawgan 2 J5
Mawnan 2 J5
Maxwellheugh 41 K10
Maybole 34 C4
Mayfield
  E Sus 10 G6
  Staffs 21 B12
Mealabost 55 D6
Mealsgate 35 J13
Measham 22 D2
Medstead 9 D11
Meidrim 12 E6
Meifod 20 E2
Meigle 51 N1
Melbourn 17 A8
Melbourne 22 C2
Melgarve 48 J5
Melksham 8 A4
Mellon Charles 46 B8
Mellor 26 B7
Melmerby 36 K5
Melrose 41 K8
Melsonby 32 D3
Meltham 27 D12
Melton 25 K7
Melton Constable . . .24 B5
Melton Mowbray 22 D6
Melvaig 46 C7
Melvich 53 B10
Menai Bridge 18 C5
Mendlesham 25 J6
Mennock 35 C9
Menston 27 A12
Menstrie 39 A13
Meonstoke 9 F11
Meopham 17 J11
Mere 8 D3
Mere Brow 26 D5
Meriden 21 H13
Merriott 5 B8
Merthyr Tydfil 13 F14
Merton 10 C3
Meshaw 6 K6
Messingham 28 D7
Metfield 24 G7
Metheringham 29 H9
Methil 40 C6
Methlick 50 D7
Methven 45 G12
Methwold 24 F2
Mevagissey 3 G8
Mexborough 28 D3
Mey 53 A14
Michaelchurch 9 D10
Michelmersh 9 E8
Mickleover 22 B2
Mickleton
  Durham 32 B1
  Glos 15 B10
Midbea 56 B4

Middle Barton 15 D13
Middleham 32 F3
Middlemarsh 5 C10
Middlesbrough 32 B7
Middleton
  Argyll 42 D1
  Grt Manchester 27 E9
  Norf 24 D1
Middleton Cheney . . .15 B14
Middleton-in-
  Teesdale 32 B1
Middleton-on-Sea . . .9 H14
Middleton on the
  Wolds 33 K11
Middlewich 26 J8
Middlezoy 7 H12
Midhurst 9 E13
Mid Lavant 9 G13
Midsomer Norton 8 B1
Mid Yell 57 C6
Milborne Port 5 B10
Mildenhall 24 H2
Milford 9 C14
Milford Haven 12 F2
Milford on Sea 8 H7
Millbrook 3 F12
Millom 30 F7
Millport 38 E6
Milnathort 40 C4
Milngavie 39 C10
Milnthorpe 31 F11
Milovaig 46 F1
Milton 48 C4
Milton Abbot 3 D11
Milton Keynes 16 B3
Milverton 7 J10
Minchinhampton 14 G7
Minehead 7 G8
Minera 20 A3
Minety 15 H9
Minnigaff 34 G5
Minster
  Kent 11 B10
  Kent 11 C14
Minsterley 20 F4
Mintlaw 50 C9
Mirfield 27 D13
Misterton
  Notts 28 E6
  Som 5 C8
Mistley 25 M6
Mitcheldean 14 E5
Mitchel Troy 14 F3
Modbury 3 F14
Moelfre 18 B5
Moffat 35 C11
Mold 26 J3
Monar Lodge 48 D3
Moniaive 35 D8
Monifieth 51 P4
Monikie 51 N4
Monkland 14 A3
Monkokehampton 3 A13
Monkton 39 H8
Monmouth 14 E4
Montacute 5 B8
Montgomery 20 G3
Montrose 51 M6
Monymusk 50 F5
Morar 47 M6
Morchard Bishop 4 C1
Mordiford 14 C4
Morebattle 36 A6
Morecambe 31 H10
Moretonhampstead . . .4 E1
Moreton-in-Marsh . . .15 C11
Morley 27 C13
Morpeth 37 E11
Mortehoe 6 E3
Mortimer's Cross 20 K5
Morwenstow 6 K1
Mossley 27 E10
Mostyn 26 H2
Motcombe 8 E3
Motherwell 39 E12
Mottisfont 9 E8
Moulton
  Lincs 23 C12
  Northants 22 J7

Moulton *continued*
  Suff 25 J2
Mountain Ash 7 B9
Mountsorrel 22 D4
Mousehole 2 J2
Mouswald 35 F11
Moy 49 E8
Muchalls 51 H7
Much Dewchurch 14 D3
Much Marcle 14 C5
Much Wenlock 20 F7
Muir 49 K11
Muirdrum 51 P4
Muirhead 39 D12
Muirkirk 39 H12
Muir of Ord 48 C6
Muker 32 E1
Mulben 50 B2
Mullion 2 K4
Mullion Cove 2 K4
Mundesley 24 B7
Mundford 24 F3
Munlochy 48 C7
Murlaggan 47 M10
Murton 37 J13
Musbury 4 D6
Musselburgh 40 F6
Muthill 45 H10
Mybster 53 C13
Myddle 20 D5
Mydroilyn 19 Q4
Mynydd Isa 26 J3

N

Nafferton 33 J12
Nailsea 7 D13
Nailsworth 14 G7
Nairn 49 C9
Nannerch 26 H2
Nantwich 20 A7
Nappa 31 J14
Narberth 12 E5
Narborough 22 F4
Naseby 22 H5
Navenby 29 J8
Neap 57 G6
Neath 13 G11
Necton 24 E3
Needham Market 25 K5
Needingworth 23 H12
Nefyn 18 G3
Neilston 39 E9
Nelson 27 B9
Nenthead 36 J6
Neston 26 H3
Netheravon 8 C6
Netherbury 5 D8
Nether Stowey 7 H10
Netherthird 34 B6
Netherton 37 C8
Nethy Bridge 49 F11
Netley 9 G9
Nettlebed 16 G2
Nettleham 29 G9
Nettleton 29 E10
Nevern 12 C4
New Abbey 35 G10
New Aberdour 50 A7
New Alresford 9 D11
Newark-on-Trent 28 J7
New Ash Green 10 C7
Newbiggin-by-the-
  Sea 37 E12
Newbigging 40 J3
Newborough 18 D4
Newbridge 7 B11
Newbridge on Wye . . .19 K8
Newbrough 36 G7
New Buckenham 24 F5
Newburgh
  Aberds 50 E8
  Fife 40 B5
Newburn 37 G10
Newbury 15 K13
Newby Bridge 31 F9
Newbyth 50 B7
Newcastle 20 H3

Newcastle Emlyn 12 C7
Newcastleton 36 E3
Newcastle-under-
  Lyme 21 B9
Newcastle-upon-
  Tyne 37 G11
Newchurch 14 A1
New Costessey 24 D6
New Cumnock 34 B7
New Deer 50 C7
Newdigate 10 E2
New Earswick 33 J8
New Edlington 28 E4
Newent 14 D6
Newgale 12 D2
New Galloway 34 F7
Newham 10 A5
Newhaven 10 J5
New Holland 29 B9
Newick 10 G5
Newington
  Kent 11 C9
  Kent 11 F12
Newlot 56 E5
New Luce 34 G2
Newlyn 2 J2
Newmachar 50 E7
Newmarket
  Suff 25 J1
  W Isles 55 D6
Newmill 50 B3
New Mills 27 G11
Newmilns 39 G10
New Milton 8 H7
Newnham 14 E5
New Pitsligo 50 B7
Newport
  Essex 17 B10
  IoW 9 J10
  Newport 7 C12
  Pembs 12 C4
  Telford 21 D8
Newport-on-Tay 40 A7
Newport Pagnell 16 A3
Newquay 2 E5
New Quay 19 Q3
New Radnor 20 K3
New Romney 11 G11
New Rossington 28 E5
New Scone 45 G13
Newton 31 J13
Newton Abbot 4 F2
Newton Arlosh 35 H12
Newton Aycliffe 32 B4
Newton Ferrers 3 G13
Newtongrange 40 G6
Newtonhill 51 H8
Newton le Willows . . .36 F6
Newton Mearns 39 E10
Newtonmore 49 J8
Newton Poppleford . . .4 E4
Newton St Cyres 4 D2
Newton Stewart 34 G5
Newtown
  Hants 8 G7
  Hereford 14 B5
  Powys 20 G2
Newtown St
  Boswells 41 K8
New Tredegar 7 A10
New Waltham 29 D11
Neyland 12 F3
Ninfield 11 H8
Niton 9 K10
Nordelph 23 E14
Norham 41 J12
Normanby le Wold . . .29 E10
Normanton 28 B3
Northallerton 32 E5
Northam 6 J3
Northampton 22 J6
North Baddesley 9 F8
North Berwick 41 E8
North Cerney 15 F9
Northchapel 9 E14
North Charlton 37 A10
North Elmham 24 C4
North Ferriby 29 B8
Northfleet 17 H11

North Frodingham . . 33 J12
North Hill 3 D10
North Hykeham 29 H8
Northiam 11 G9
North Kessock 48 D7
Northleach 15 E10
North Molton 6 J6
North Newbald 29 A8
Northop 26 J3
North Petherton 7 H11
Northpunds 57 K5
North Queensferry . . 40 E4
Northrepps 24 B7
North Somercotes . . 29 E13
North Tawton 3 B14
North Thoresby 29 E11
North Walsham 24 B7
Northwich 26 H7
North Wingfield 28 H3
Northwold 24 F2
Northwood
  IoW 9 H9
  London 16 F5
Norton
  Glos 14 D7
  N Yorks 33 G9
  Suff 25 J4
  Worcs 14 A7
Norton Fitzwarren . . 7 J10
Norwich 24 E7
Norwick 57 A7
Nottingham 22 B4
Nuneaton 22 F2
Nunney 8 C2
Nutley 10 G5
Nybster 53 B15

O

Oadby 22 E5
Oakdale 7 B10
Oakengates 21 E8
Oakham 22 E7
Oakley 40 E3
Oban 42 E10
Ochiltree 34 A6
Ockley 10 F2
Odie 56 D6
Odiham 9 C12
Offord D'Arcy 23 J11
Ogbourne St
  George 15 J10
Okehampton 3 B13
Old Basing 9 B11
Old Bolingbroke . . 29 H12
Oldbury 14 G5
Old Colwyn 18 C8
Old Deer 50 C8
Old Fletton 23 F10
Oldham 27 E10
Old Leake 29 K12
Oldmeldrum 50 E7
Old Radnor 14 A1
Olgrinmore 53 C12
Ollaberry 57 D4
Ollerton 28 H5
Olney 22 K7
Ombersley 21 K9
Onchan 30 H3
Onich 44 C2
Opinan 46 B8
Ordhead 50 F5
Ordie 50 G3
Orford 25 K9
Orleton 20 K6
Ormesby St
  Margaret 24 D9
Ormiston 40 G7
Ormskirk 26 D5
Orpington 10 C5
Orton 31 D12
Osbournby 23 B9
Oskamull 42 D6
Osmotherley 32 E6
Ossett 27 D13
Oswaldtwistle 27 C8
Oswestry 20 D3
Otford 10 D6

Othery 7 H12
Otley 32 K3
Otterburn 36 D7
Otter Ferry 38 B4
Otterton 4 E4
Ottery St Mary 4 D4
Oulton 24 F10
Oulton Broad 24 F10
Oundle 23 G9
Ousdale 53 G12
Outwell 23 E14
Over 23 H12
Overbister 56 B6
Overseal 21 E13
Overstrand 24 B7
Overton
  Hants 9 C10
  Wrex 20 B4
Over Wallop 8 D7
Owston Ferry 28 E7
Oxenholme 31 F11
Oxford 15 F14
Oxnam 36 B6
Oxted 10 D4
Oykel Bridge 52 H5

P

Pabail 55 D7
Paddock Wood 10 E7
Padiham 27 B9
Padstow 2 D7
Paibeil 54 C4
Paignton 4 H2
Pailton 22 G3
Painscastle 13 B15
Painshawfield 37 H9
Painswick 14 F7
Paisley 39 D9
Palgrave 24 H6
Palnackie 35 H9
Pangbourne 16 H1
Papworth Everard . . 23 J11
Parkeston 25 M7
Parkhurst 9 H9
Parracombe 6 G5
Partney 29 H13
Parton 30 B5
Pateley Bridge 32 H3
Pathhead 40 G7
Patna 34 B5
Patrick Brompton . . 32 E4
Patrington 29 B12
Patterdale 31 C9
Paull 29 B10
Paulton 8 B1
Peacehaven 10 J5
Peak Forest 27 H12
Peasedown St John . . 8 B2
Peasenhall 25 J8
Peasmarsh 11 G10
Peebles 40 J5
Peel 30 G2
Pegswood 37 E11
Peinchorran 47 H5
Pembrey 12 F8
Pembridge 14 A3
Pembroke 12 F3
Pembroke Dock . . . 12 F3
Pembury 10 F7
Penally 12 G5
Penarth 7 D10
Pencader 12 C8
Pencoed 13 H13
Pendeen 2 C4
Penderyn 13 F13
Pendine 12 F6
Penicuik 40 G5
Penistone 27 E13
Penkridge 21 E10
Penmachno 18 F7
Penmaenmawr 18 C7
Pennan 50 A7
Pennyghael 42 F7
Penpont 35 D9
Penrhyndeudraeth . . 18 G6
Penrith 31 A11
Penryn 2 H5

Pensford 8 A1
Penshaw 37 H12
Penshurst 10 E6
Pensilva 3 E10
Pentraeth 18 C5
Pentrefoelas 18 E8
Penybont 20 K2
Pen-y-gop 18 F9
Penybontfawr 20 D1
Penygroes
  Carms 13 E9
  Gwyn 18 E4
Penysarn 18 B4
Penzance 2 J2
Perranporth 2 F5
Perranzabuloe 2 G5
Pershore 15 B8
Perth 45 G13
Peterborough 23 F10
Peterchurch 14 C2
Peterculter 50 G7
Peterhead 50 C10
Peterlee 37 J13
Petersfield 9 E12
Petworth 9 E14
Pevensey 10 J7
Pewsey 8 B6
Pickering 33 F9
Piddletrenthide 5 D11
Pidley 23 H12
Pierowall 56 B4
Pilling 31 K10
Pilton 7 H14
Pinchbeck 23 C11
Pinhoe 4 D3
Pinmore Mains 34 D3
Pinwherry 34 E3
Pirbright 9 B14
Pirnmill 38 F3
Pitlochry 45 D11
Pittenweem 41 C8
Plean 39 B13
Plockton 47 H8
Pluckley 11 E10
Plumpton 36 K4
Plymouth 3 F12
Plympton 3 F13
Plymstock 3 F13
Pocklington 33 K10
Polegate 10 J6
Polesworth 21 F13
Polloch 42 B10
Polperro 3 G9
Polruan 3 G9
Polwarth 41 H10
Polzeath 2 D7
Pontardawe 13 F11
Pontardulais 13 F9
Pontefract 28 B3
Ponteland 37 F10
Ponterwyd 19 M7
Pontesbury 20 F5
Pontrhydfendigaid . . 19 P7
Pontrilas 14 D3
Pontyates 13 F8
Pontyberem 13 E8
Pontypool 7 A11
Pontypridd 7 C9
Pool 2 G4
Poole 8 J5
Poolewe 46 D8
Pooley Bridge 31 B10
Porlock 6 G7
Port Appin 44 E1
Portavadie 38 C4
Port Bannatyne . . . 38 D5
Port Carlisle 35 G13
Port Charlotte 43 N4
Port Ellen 43 P5
Portencross 38 F6
Port Erin 30 J2
Port Eynon 13 H8
Port Glasgow 39 C8
Portgordon 50 A2
Porth 7 B9
Porthcawl 13 J12
Port Henderson . . . 46 D7
Porthleven 2 J4

Porthmadog 18 G5
Port Isaac 2 D7
Portishead 14 J3
Portknockie 50 A3
Portlethen 51 H8
Port Logan 34 J2
Portmahomack 53 K11
Portnacroish 44 E1
Portnahaven 43 N3
Portnalong 47 H3
Port Nan Giuran . . . 55 D7
Port Nan Long 54 B6
Port Nis 55 A7
Porton 8 D6
Portpatrick 34 H1
Port Ramsay 42 D10
Portreath 2 G4
Portree 46 G4
Port St Mary 30 J2
Portskerra 53 B10
Portslade-by-Sea . . 10 J3
Portsmouth 9 H11
Portsoy 50 A4
Port Talbot 13 H11
Port William 34 J4
Postbridge 3 D14
Potter Heigham . . . 24 D9
Potterne 8 B4
Potters Bar 16 E7
Potterspury 16 A2
Potton 16 A7
Poulton-le-Fylde . . 26 B4
Poundstock 3 B9
Powick 14 A7
Poynton 27 G10
Praa Sands 2 J3
Prees 20 C6
Preesall 31 K9
Presbury 27 H10
Prescot 26 F5
Prestatyn 26 G1
Prestbury 15 D8
Presteigne 20 K4
Preston
  Borders 41 H10
  Dorset 5 E10
  E Yorks 29 A10
  Kent 11 C13
  Lancs 26 B6
Preston Candover . . 9 C11
Prestonpans 40 F6
Prestwich 27 E9
Prestwick 34 A4
Prestwood 16 E3
Princes Risborough . . 16 E3
Princetown 3 D13
Probus 2 G6
Prudhoe 37 G9
Pubil 44 E6
Pucklechurch 14 J5
Puddletown 5 D11
Pudsey 27 B13
Pulborough 10 H1
Pulham Market 24 G6
Pulham St Mary . . . 24 G7
Pumpsaint 13 B10
Purfleet 17 H10
Purley
  London 10 C4
  W Berks 16 H1
Purton 15 H9
Puttenham 9 C14
Pwllheli 18 G3
Pyle 13 H12

Q

Quadring 23 B11
Quainton 16 D2
Quedgeley 14 F7
Queenborough 11 B10
Queensbury 27 C12
Queensferry
  Edin 40 F4
  Flint 26 J4
Quorndon 22 D4

Nor–Ric 73

R

Rackenford 4 B2
Rackheath 24 D7
Rackwick 56 G2
Radcliffe 27 E8
Radcliffe-on-Trent . . 22 B5
Radlett 16 F6
Radley 15 G14
Radstock 8 B1
Radyr 7 C10
Raglan 14 F3
Rainham 11 C9
Rainworth 28 J5
Rampisde 31 H8
Rampside 31 H8
Ramsbottom 27 D8
Ramsey
  Cambs 23 G11
  Essex 25 M7
  IoM 30 F4
Ramseycleuch 35 B13
Ramsgate 11 C14
Rannoch Station . . 44 D6
Rapness 56 B5
Rathen 50 A9
Rattray 45 E13
Raunds 23 H8
Ravenglass 30 E6
Ravenshead 28 J4
Ravenstonedale . . . 31 D13
Rawcliffe 32 J7
Rawmarsh 28 E3
Rawtenstall 27 C9
Rayleigh 17 F13
Reading 16 H2
Reay 53 B11
Redbourn 16 D6
Redbridge 17 G9
Redcar 33 B8
Red Dial 35 J13
Redditch 21 K11
Reedsmouth 36 E7
Redhill 10 E3
Red Houses . . . . 5 Jersey
Redland 56 D3
Redlynch 8 F7
Redmile 22 B7
Redmire 32 E2
Red Point 46 E7
Redruth 2 G4
Reedham 24 E9
Reepham 24 C5
Reeth 32 E2
Reigate 10 E3
Reiss 53 C15
Renfrew 39 D10
Rennington 37 B11
Repton 22 C2
Resolven 13 F12
Reston 41 G11
Retford 28 F6
Reydon 24 H10
Rhayader 19 P9
Rhewl 26 J2
Rhiconich 52 C4
Rhiw 18 H2
Rhonehouse 13 G13
Rhoose 7 E9
Rhoslan 18 F4
Rhosllanerchrugog . . 20 B3
Rhosneigr 18 C3
Rhos-on-Sea 18 B8
Rhossili 12 H8
Rhostryfan 18 E4
Rhubodach 38 C5
Rhuddlan 18 C10
Rhyd-Ddu 18 E5
Rhyl 18 B10
Rhymney 13 F15
Rhynie 50 E3
Riccall 28 A5
Richmond
  London 10 B2
  N Yorks 32 D3

74 Ric–Spi

Rickmansworth 16 F5
Ridsdale 37 E8
Rievaulx 32 F7
Rigside 39 G13
Rillington 33 G10
Ringford 34 H7
Ringmer 10 H5
Ringwood 8 G6
Ripley
  Derbys 28 J3
  N Yorks 32 H4
  Sur 10 D1
Ripon 32 G5
Ripponden 27 C11
Risca 7 C11
Rishton 27 B8
Roade 22 K6
Roadhead 36 F4
Roberton 36 B3
Robertsbridge 11 G8
Robin Hood's Bay .. 33 D11
Rocester 21 C12
Rochdale 27 D9
Roche 2 F7
Rochester
  Medway 17 J12
  Northumb 36 D7
Rochford 17 G13
Rockcliffe
  Cumb 36 G2
  Dumfries 35 H9
Rockingham 22 F7
Rogart 53 H9
Rogate 9 E13
Roghadal 55 J2
Rolvenden 11 F9
Romford 17 G10
Romsey 9 E8
Ropsley 23 B9
Rosedale Abbey 33 E9
Rosehall 52 H6
Rosehearty 50 A8
Rosemarket 12 F3
Rosemarkie 49 C8
Roskhill 46 G2
Roslin 40 G5
Rosneath 38 B7
Ross 41 K14
Rossett 26 K4
Ross-On-Wye 14 D5
Rosyth 40 E4
Rothbury 37 C9
Rotherham 28 E3
Rothes 49 D13
Rothesay 38 D5
Rothienorman 50 D6
Rothiesholm 56 D6
Rothwell
  Northants 22 G7
  W Yorks 28 B2
Rottal 51 K2
Rottingdean 10 J4
Rowanburn 36 F3
Rowlands Gill 37 H10
Roxburgh 41 K10
Roxby 29 C8
Royal Leamington
  Spa 22 J2
Royal Tunbridge
  Wells 10 F6
Royal Wootton
  Bassett 15 H9
Roybridge 44 A4
Royston
  Herts 17 A8
  S Yorks 28 D2
Royton 27 E10
Ruabon 20 B4
Ruan Minor 2 K5
Ruardean 14 E5
Rubery 21 J10
Rudston 33 H12
Rufford 26 D5
Rugby 22 H4
Rugeley 21 E11
Ruislip 16 G6

Rumburgh 24 G8
Rumney 7 D11
Runcorn 26 G6
Rushden 23 J8
Rushwick 14 A7
Ruskington 29 J9
Rutherglen 39 D11
Ruthin 26 K2
Ruthven 49 H8
Ruthwell 35 G11
Ryal 37 F9
Rydal 31 D9
Ryde 9 H10
Rye 11 G10
Ryhall 23 D9
Ryhope 37 H13
Ryton 22 H2

S

Sacriston 37 J11
Saddell 38 G2
Saffron Walden 17 B10
Sageston 12 F4
St Abb's 41 G12
St Agnes 2 G5
St Albans 16 E6
St Andrews 41 B8
St Ann's 35 D11
St Arvans 14 G4
St Asaph 18 C10
St Athan 7 E9
St Aubin .... 5 Jersey
St Austell 3 F8
St Bees 30 C5
St Blazey 3 F8
St Breward 3 D8
St Briavels 14 F4
St Bride's Major .. 13 J12
St Buryan 2 J1
St Clears 12 E6
St Columb Major ... 2 E6
St Columb Minor ... 2 E6
St Combs 50 A9
St Cyrus 51 L6
St David's 12 D1
St Day 2 G5
St Dennis 2 F7
St Dogmaels 12 B5
St Dominick 3 E11
St Enoder 2 F6
St Erth 2 H3
St Fergus 50 B9
St Fillans 45 G8
St Germans 3 F11
St Harmon 19 N9
St Helens 26 F6
St Helier .... 5 Jersey
St Issey 2 D7
St Ives
  Cambs 23 H12
  Corn 2 H3
St John's
  IoM 30 G2
  Jersey .... 5 Jersey
St Johns Chapel ... 31 A14
St John's Town of
  Dalry 34 E7
St Just 2 H1
St Keverne 2 K5
St Leonards 11 J9
St Levan 2 J1
St Mabyn 3 D8
St Margaret's-at-
  Cliffe 11 E14
St Margaret's Hope . 56 G4
St Martin's .... 5 Jersey
St Mary Bourne 9 B9
St Mary's 56 F4
St Mary's Bay 11 G11
St Mawes 2 H6
St Mellons 7 D11
St Merryn 2 D6
St Minver 2 D7
St Monance 41 C8
St Neots 23 J10
St Newlyn East 2 F6
St Olaves 24 F9

St Osyth 25 P6
St Ouens .... 5 Jersey
St Peter Port ..... 4 Guern
St Peter's .... 5 Jersey
St Sampson .... 4 Guern
St Stephen 2 F7
St Teath 3 D8
St Tudy 3 D8
Salcombe 4 K1
Sale 27 F8
Salen
  Argyll 42 D7
  Highland 42 B8
Salford 27 F9
Salford Priors 15 A9
Saline 40 D3
Salisbury 8 E6
Sallachy 52 H7
Saltash 3 F12
Saltburn-by-the-
  Sea 33 B8
Saltcoats 38 F7
Saltfleet 29 E13
Saltfleetby 29 E13
Saltwood 11 F12
Sampford Courtenay . 3 B14
Sanaigmore 43 L4
Sandbach 27 J8
Sandbank 38 C6
Sandgate 11 F13
Sandhead 34 J2
Sandhurst 16 J3
Sandleigh 15 F13
Sandness 57 G2
Sandown 9 J10
Sandringham 24 B1
Sandwich 11 D14
Sandy 16 A6
Sanquhar 35 B8
Sarnau 12 A7
Sarnesfield 14 A2
Sarre 11 C13
Satterthwaite 31 E9
Saundersfoot 12 F5
Sawbridgeworth 17 D9
Sawston 17 A9
Sawtry 23 G10
Saxilby 29 G8
Saxlingham
  Nethergate 24 F7
Saxmundham 25 J8
Saxthorpe 24 B6
Scalasaig 43 J5
Scalby 33 F12
Scalloway 57 J4
Scalpay 55 H4
Scamblesby 29 G11
Scarborough 33 F12
Scardoy 48 C3
Scarinish 42 D2
Scarning 24 D4
Scole 24 H6
Sconser 47 H5
Scopwick 29 J9
Scorton 32 D4
Scotch Corner 32 D4
Scotter 28 D7
Scourie 52 D3
Scousburgh 57 L4
Scrabster 53 B13
Scremerston 41 J13
Scunthorpe 28 C7
Seaford 10 K5
Seaham 37 J13
Seahouses 41 K15
Seamer 33 F12
Sea Palling 24 C9
Seascale 30 D6
Seaton
  Cumb 30 A6
  Devon 4 E6
Seaton Delaval 37 F12
Seaview 9 H11
Sebergham 36 J2
Sedbergh 31 E12
Sedgefield 32 A5
Seend 8 B4
Selborne 9 D12
Selby 28 A5

Selkirk 36 A3
Sellafield 30 D6
Selsey 9 H13
Sennen 2 J1
Sennybridge 13 D13
Settle 31 H14
Sevenoaks 10 D6
Seven Sisters 13 F12
Severn Beach 14 H4
Severn Stoke 14 B7
Sgarasta Mhor 55 H2
Sgiogarstaigh 55 A7
Shaftesbury 8 E3
Shalcombe 9 J8
Shaldon 4 F3
Shalford 9 C15
Shanklin 9 J10
Shap 31 C11
Sharnbrook 23 J8
Sharpness 14 F5
Shawbury 20 D6
Shawford 9 E9
Shebbear 3 A12
Sheerness 11 B10
Sheffield 28 F2
Shefford 16 B6
Sheigra 52 B3
Shenfield 17 F11
Shepley 27 D12
Shepshed 22 D3
Shepton Mallet 8 C1
Sherborne 5 B10
Sherborne St John . 9 B11
Sherburn 33 G11
Sherburn in Elmet . 28 A3
Shere 10 E1
Sherfield English . 8 E7
Sherfield on Loddon . 9 B11
Sheriff Hutton 33 H8
Sheringham 24 A6
Sherston 14 H7
Shiel Bridge 47 K9
Shieldaig 46 F8
Shifnal 21 F8
Shilbottle 37 C10
Shildon 32 B4
Shillingstone 8 G3
Shillington 16 B6
Shinfield 16 J2
Shipdham 24 E4
Shipley 27 B12
Shipston-on-Stour 15 C11
Shipton under
  Wychwood 15 E11
Shirebrook 28 H4
Shoeburyness 17 G14
Shoreham-by-Sea ... 10 J3
Shorwell 9 J9
Shotley Bridge 37 H10
Shotley Gate 25 M7
Shottermill 9 D13
Shottisham 25 L8
Shotts 39 D13
Shrewsbury 20 E5
Shrewton 8 C5
Shrivenham 15 H11
Siabost 55 C4
Sible Hedingham ... 25 M2
Sibsey 29 J12
Sidbury 4 E5
Sidford 4 E5
Sidlesham 9 H13
Sidmouth 4 E5
Silloth 35 H12
Silsden 32 K2
Silverdale 31 G10
Silverstone 16 A1
Silverton 4 C3
Simonsbath 3 H6
Singleton 9 F13
Sittingbourne 11 C10
Sixpenny Handley .. 8 F5
Sizewell 25 J9
Skegness 29 H14
Skellingthorpe ... 29 G8
Skelmersdale 26 E5
Skelmorlie 38 D6
Skelton
  Cumb 31 A10

Skelton continued
  Redcar 33 C8
Skerray 52 B8
Skinburness 35 H12
Skipness 38 E4
Skipsea 33 J13
Skipton 32 J1
Skirlaugh 29 A10
Slaidburn 31 J13
Slaithwaite 27 D11
Slaley 37 H8
Slamannan 39 C13
Sleaford 23 A9
Sledmere 33 H11
Sleights 33 D10
Sligachan 47 H4
Slough 16 H4
Smailholm 41 K9
Smarden 11 E9
Smethwick 21 H11
Smithfield 36 G3
Snainton 33 F11
Snaith 28 B5
Snape 25 K8
Sneaton 33 D10
Snettisham 24 B1
Snodland 17 J12
Soham 23 H14
Solas 54 B5
Solihull 21 H12
Solva 12 D1
Somerby 22 D6
Somercotes 28 J3
Somersham 23 H12
Somerton 7 J13
Sonning 16 H2
Sonning Common ... 16 H2
Sopley 8 H6
Sorbie 34 J5
Sordale 53 B13
Sorisdale 42 B4
Sorn 39 H10
Sortat 53 B14
Soulby 31 C13
Southam 22 J3
Southampton 9 F9
South Anston 28 F4
South Benfleet ... 17 G12
Southborough 10 E6
South Brent 9 F14
South Cave 29 A8
South Cerney 15 G9
South Elkington .. 29 F11
Southend 38 K1
Southend-on-Sea .. 17 G13
Southery 24 F1
South Harting 9 F13
South Hayling 9 H12
South Kelsey 29 E9
South Kirkby 28 C3
Southminster 17 F14
South Molton 6 J5
South Ockendon ... 17 G10
South Otterington . 32 F5
South Petherton ... 5 B8
South Petherwin ... 3 C11
Southport 26 D4
South Shields 37 G12
South Tawton 3 B14
South Walsham 24 D8
Southwark 10 B4
South Warnborough 9 C12
Southwell 28 J5
Southwick 10 J3
Southwold 24 H10
South Woodham
  Ferrers 17 F13
South Wootton 24 C1
South Zeal 3 B14
Sowerby 32 F6
Sowerby Bridge ... 27 C11
Spalding 23 C11
Spaldwick 23 H10
Sparkford 5 A10
Spean Bridge 44 A4
Speke 26 G5
Spennymoor 32 A4
Spey Bay 50 A2
Spilsby 29 H13

Spittal 12 D3
Spittal of Glenmuick. 51 J1
Spittle of Glenshee . 45 B12
Spixworth 24 D7
Spofforth 32 J5
Spott 41 F9
Sproatley 29 A10
Stadhampton 16 F1
Staffin 46 E4
Stafford 21 D10
Staindrop 32 B3
Staines-upon-
    Thames 16 H5
Stainforth
    N Yorks 31 H14
    S Yorks 28 C5
Stainton
    Lincs. 29 G9
    Mbro. 32 C6
Staintondale 33 E11
Staithes 33 C9
Stalbridge 5 B11
Stalham 24 C8
Stallingborough 29 C10
Stalybridge 27 F10
Stamford 23 E9
Stamford Bridge . . 33 J9
Stamfordham 37 F9
Standish 26 D6
Standlake. 15 F12
Stanford le Hope . .17 G12
Stanford on Teme . .21 K8
Stanhope 37 K8
Stanley
    Durham 37 H11
    Perth 45 F13
Stannington 37 F11
Stansted Airport. . . .17 C10
Stansted
    Mountfitchet 17 C10
Stanton 25 H4
Stanton Harcourt . . .15 F14
Stanton St John 15 F14
Stanway 15 C9
Stanwix 36 H3
Stapleford 22 B3
Staplehurst 11 E8
Starcross 4 F3
Staunton 14 D6
Staunton on Wye . . .14 B2
Staveley
    Cumb 31 E10
    Derbys 28 G3
Staxigoe 53 C15
Staxton 33 G12
Steeple Bumpstead 17 A11
Steeple Claydon 16 C2
Stein 46 F2
Stenhousemuir 39 B13
Stenness 57 E3
Stevenage 16 C7
Stevenston 38 F7
Stewarton 39 F9
Steyning 10 H2
Stibb Cross 6 J9
Stichill 41 K10
Stickford 29 H12
Stickney 29 J12
Stillington 32 H7
Stilton 23 G10
Stirling 39 A12
Stobbs 36 C4
Stobo 40 K4
Stock. 17 F12
Stockbridge. 9 D8
Stockport. 27 F10
Stocksbridge. 27 F13
Stockton. 22 J3
Stockton-on-Tees . . 32 B6
Stoer 52 F2
Stoke. 11 B9
Stoke Albany 22 G7
Stoke Ferry 24 F2
Stoke Fleming 4 J2
Stoke Gabriel 4 H2
Stoke Mandeville . . .16 E3
Stokenchurch 16 F2
Stoke-on-Trent 21 B9
Stoke Poges 16 G4

Stoke Prior 21 K10
Stokesley 32 C7
Stone
    Bucks 16 D2
    Glos 14 G5
    Staffs 21 C9
Stonehaven 51 J7
Stonehouse
    Glos 14 F7
    S Lanark 39 F12
Stoneykirk 34 H2
Stonham Aspal 25 K6
Stony Stratford 16 B3
Stornoway 55 D6
Storrington 10 H1
Stotfold. 16 B7
Stourbridge. 21 H10
Stourpaine. 8 G3
Stourport-on-
    Severn 21 J9
Stow 40 J7
Stow Bardolph 24 E1
Stowmarket. 25 K5
Stow-on-the-Wold 15 D11
Strachan. 51 H5
Strachur 44 J2
Stradbroke. 25 H7
Straiton 34 C4
Stratford St Mary . . 25 M5
Stratford-upon-
    Avon 15 A11
Strathan 52 B7
Strathaven 39 F11
Strathblane 39 C10
Strathdon 50 F2
Strathkanaird 52 H3
Strathpeffer. 48 C5
Strathy 53 B10
Strathyre 44 H7
Stratmiglo 40 B5
Stratton
    Corn 3 A10
    Glos 15 F9
Stratton St
    Margaret 15 H10
Streatley. 15 J14
Street 7 H13
Strensall 33 H8
Stretford. 27 F9
Stretham 23 H14
Stretton
    Rutland. 23 D8
    Staffs 21 D13
    Warr. 26 G7
Strichen 50 B8
Stromeferry 47 H8
Stromemore 47 H8
Stromness 56 E2
Stronachlachar. 44 H6
Strone. 38 B6
Strontian 42 B10
Stroud 14 F7
Struy 48 D4
Stubbington 9 G10
Studland. 8 J5
Studley 21 K11
Sturminster Marshall . 8 H4
Sturminster Newton . 5 B11
Sturry 11 D12
Sturton 28 F7
Sudbury
    Derbys 21 C12
    Suff. 25 L3
Sulby 30 F3
Sullom 57 E4
Sully 7 G10
Sumburgh 57 M5
Sunderland. 37 H13
Sunk Island 29 C11
Sunninghill 16 J4
Sutterton 23 B11
Sutton
    Cambs 23 H13
    London 10 C3
Sutton Bridge 24 D1
Sutton Coldfield 21 G12
Sutton Courtenay. . .15 G14
Sutton-in-Ashfield . .28 H3

Sutton Lane Ends. . .27 H10
Sutton-on-Sea. 29 F14
Sutton-on-Trent 28 H6
Sutton Scotney. 9 D9
Sutton-under-
    Whitestonecliffe . . 32 F6
Sutton Valence 11 E9
Swadlincote 21 E13
Swaffham. 24 E3
Swalcliffe. 15 C12
Swaleclffe. 11 C12
Swanage 8 K5
Swanley 10 C6
Swansea. 13 G10
Swanton 28 C5
Sway 8 H7
Swindon 15 H10
Swinefleet 28 B6
Swineshead 23 A11
Swinton
    Borders 41 J11
    Grt Manchester . . .27 E8
    S Yorks 28 E3
Symbister. 57 F6
Symington 40 K2
Symonds Yat 14 E4
Syresham 16 A1
Syston 22 D5

T

Tadcaster 32 K6
Tadley 9 A11
Talgarth 13 C15
Taliesin 13 C10
Talsarnau 18 G6
Talybont 19 M6
Tal-y-llyn. 19 K7
Talysarn 18 E4
Tamerton Foliot 3 F12
Tamworth. 21 F13
Tangmere. 9 G13
Tannadice 51 M3
Tanworth-in-Arden 21 J12
Taobh Tuath 55 J1
Tarbert / Aird Asaig
    Tairbeart 55 G3
Tarbet
    Argyll 44 J5
    Highland. 47 M7
Tarbolton 39 H9
Tarland 50 G3
Tarleton 26 C5
Tarporley 26 J6
Tarrant Hinton 8 G4
Tarskavaig 47 K5
Tarves 50 D7
Tarvin 26 J5
Tattenhall. 26 K5
Tattersett 24 B3
Taunton 7 J11
Tavistock 3 D12
Tay Bridge 40 A7
Tayinloan 38 F2
Taynuilt 44 F2
Tayport 40 A7
Teangue 47 L6
Tebay 31 D12
Tedburn St Mary . . . 4 D2
Teesside 32 B6
Teignmouth 4 F3
Telford 20 F7
Temple Combe 5 A11
Temple Ewell 11 E13
Temple Sowerby . . .31 B12
Templeton 12 E5
Tenbury Wells 20 K7
Tenby 12 G5
Tenterden 11 F9
Terrington 33 G8
Terrington St
    Clement 23 C14
Tetbury 14 G7
Tetney 29 D12
Tetsworth 16 E1
Teviothead 36 C3

Tewkesbury 15 C8
Teynham. 11 C10
Thame. 16 E2
Thatcham. 15 K14
Thaxted 17 B11
Theale 16 H1
The Barony 56 D2
The Mumbles 13 H10
Thetford 24 G3
Thirsk 32 F6
Thornaby on Tees. . .32 C6
Thornbury 14 H5
Thorndon 25 J6
Thorne 28 C5
Thorney 23 E11
Thornham 24 A2
Thornhill
    Dumfries 35 D9
    Stirling 45 J8
Thornthwaite 31 B8
Thornton 26 A4
Thornton-le-Dale . . 33 F10
Thorpe 24 F7
Thorpe-le-Soken . . .25 N6
Thorverton 4 C3
Thrapston 23 H8
Three Legged Cross . 8 G5
Threlkeld 31 B9
Threshfield 32 H1
Thrumster 53 D15
Thurcroft 28 F3
Thurlby 23 D10
Thurlestone 3 G14
Thurmaston 22 E5
Thursby 36 H2
Thurso 53 B13
Ticehurst 11 G8
Tickhill 28 E4
Tideswell 27 H12
Tidworth. 8 C7
Tighnabruaich 38 C4
Tilbury 17 H11
Tillicoultry 40 D2
Tillington 17 E15
Tilmanstone 11 E13
Timberscombe 7 G8
Timsbury 8 B1
Tingewick 16 B1
Tingwall 56 D3
Tintagel 3 C8
Tintern Parva 14 F4
Tipton 21 G10
Tiptree 25 P4
Tisbury 8 E4
Titchfield 9 G10
Tiverton 4 B3
Toab. 57 L4
Tollesbury 25 Q4
Tolleshunt D'Arcy . . . 5 D11
Tolpuddle 5 D11
Tomatin 49 F9
Tomdoun 48 H2
Tomintoul 49 G12
Tomnavoulin 49 F13
Tonbridge 10 E6
Tondu 13 H12
Tong 21 F9
Tongue 52 C7
Tonyrefail 7 C9
Topcliffe 32 G6
Topsham. 4 E3
Torbay. 4 H3
Torcross 4 J2
Torness 48 F6
Torphins 50 G5
Torpoint 3 F12
Torquay. 4 G3
Torridon 46 F9
Torroble 52 F7
Torthorwald. 35 E11
Torver 31 E8
Toscaig 47 H7
Totland 9 J8

Totley 28 F2
Totnes 4 H1
Totton 9 F8
Towcester 16 A2
Tow Law 37 K10
Town Yetholm 36 A7
Trafford Park. 27 F8
Tranent 40 F7
Trawsfynydd 18 G7
Trecastle. 13 D12
Tredegar. 13 F15
Trefeglwys 19 L9
Trefnant 18 C10
Trefriw 18 D7
Tregaron. 19 Q6
Tregony. 2 G7
Tregynon 20 G2
Treharris. 7 B10
Trelech 12 C6
Tremadog. 18 G5
Trenance 2 E6
Trentham 21 B9
Treorchy 13 G13
Tresilian 2 G6
Tretower. 13 D15
Treuddyn 26 K3
Trimdon 32 A5
Trimley 25 M7
Tring 16 D4
Trinity . . . . .5 Jersey
Troon 39 G8
Troutbeck 31 D10
Trowbridge 8 B3
Trull 7 J11
Trumpan 46 E2
Trumpington 23 K13
Trunch 24 B7
Truro 2 G6
Tuddenham 25 H2
Tudweiliog 18 G2
Tullynessle. 50 F4
Tummel Bridge. 45 D9
Tunstall. 25 K8
Turnberry. 34 C3
Turriff 50 B6
Turvey 23 K8
Tutbury 21 D13
Tuxford 28 G6
Twatt 56 D2
Tweedmouth. 41 H12
Tweedshaws 35 B11
Tweedsmuir. 35 A11
Twenty 23 C10
Twyford
    Hants 9 E9
    Leics. 22 D6
    Wokingham 16 H3
Tydd St Giles 23 D13
Tydd St Mary 23 D13
Tylorstown 7 B9
Tyndrum. 44 F5
Tynemouth 37 G12
Ty'n-y-groes. 18 C7
Tywardreath 3 F8
Tywyn 19 K5

U

Uckfield 10 G5
Uddingston 39 D11
Uffculme 4 B4
Uffington 15 H12
Ufford 25 K8
Ugborough 3 F14
Uig. 46 E4
Ulbster 53 D15
Ulceby 29 C9
Ulceby Cross 29 G13
Uley 14 G6
Ullapool 52 J3
Ulsta 57 D5
Ulverston 31 G8
Unapool 52 E4
Upavon 8 B6

Uphill 7 F12
Upper Chapel 13 C14
Upper Heyford 15 D14
Upper Hindhope. . . . 36 C6
Upper Poppleton . . . 32 J7
Upper Tean. 21 C11
Uppertown. 56 G4
Uppingham 22 F7
Upton 26 J5
Upton Snodsbury . . 15 A8
Upton upon Severn . 14 B7
Upwey. 5 E10
Urchfont. 8 B5
Urmston. 27 F8
Usk. 14 F2
Usselby. 29 E9
Uttoxeter 21 C11
Uyeasound. 57 B6

V

Valley 18 C2
Veness 56 C5
Ventnor. 9 K10
Verwood. 8 G5
Veryan. 2 H7
Vickerstown. 30 H7
Vidlin. 57 F5
Virginia Water. 16 J5
Voe. 57 F5
Voy. 56 E2

W

Waddesdon 16 D2
Waddingham. 29 E8
Waddington. 29 H8
Wadebridge. 2 D7
Wadhurst 10 F7
Wainfleet All
  Saints. 29 H13
Wakefield. 28 B2
Walberswick. 25 H9
Walcott. 29 J10
Walderslade. 17 J12
Waldron. 10 H6
Walford. 20 J4
Walkerburn 40 K6
Walkeringham. 28 E6
Wallasey. 26 F4
Wallingford. 16 G1
Walls. 57 H3
Wallsend. 37 G12
Walmer. 11 E14
Walpole. 23 D13
Walsall. 21 G11
Walsham le Willows .25 H4
Walsoken. 23 D13
Waltham. 29 D11
Waltham Abbey . . . 17 F8
Waltham Forest . . . 17 G8
Waltham on the
  Wolds. 22 C7
Walton 36 G4
Walton-on-Thames .10 C2
Walton-on-the-
  Naze. 25 N7
Wanborough 15 H11
Wandsworth 10 B3
Wangford. 24 H9
Wansford. 23 F9
Wantage. 15 H13
Warboys. 23 G12
Wardington. 15 B13
Wardle. 26 K7
Ware. 17 D8
Wareham. 8 J4
Wargrave. 16 H2
Wark. 36 F7
Warkworth. 37 C11
Warley. 21 H11
Warminster. 8 C3

Warrington 26 G7
Warton 31 G10
Warwick 22 J1
Wasbister. 56 C3
Washaway 3 E8
Washford 7 H9
Washingborough. . . . 29 G9
Washington
  T&W. 37 H12
  W Sus. 10 H2
Watchet 7 G9
Watchfield. 15 G11
Waterbeach. 23 J13
Waterhead. 51 K3
Waterhouses. 21 A11
Wateringbury 10 D7
Waterlooville. 9 G11
Watford. 16 F6
Wath upon Dearne . 28 E3
Watlington
  Norf 24 D1
  Oxon. 16 F1
Watten 53 C14
Watton 24 E4
Waunfawr 18 E5
Weachyburn 50 B5
Wearhead. 36 K7
Weasenham. 24 C3
Weaverham. 26 H7
Weaverthorpe. . . . 33 G11
Wedmore. 7 G13
Wednesbury 21 G10
Wednesfield. 21 F10
Weedon Bec 22 J5
Weeley 25 N6
Welbourn 29 J8
Weldon
  Northants. 23 G8
  Northumb. 37 D10
Welford
  Northants. 22 G5
  W Berks 15 J13
Wellesbourne. 15 A11
Wellingborough . . . 22 J7
Wellington
  Som 4 B5
  Telford 20 E7
Wells. 7 G14
Wells-next-the-Sea .24 A4
Welney 23 F14
Welshampton 20 C5
Welshpool. 20 F3
Welton 29 G9
Welwyn Garden City .16 D7
Wem. 20 D6
Wembury 3 G13
Wemyss Bay 38 C6
Wendover. 16 E3
Wensley 32 E3
Wenvoe 7 D10
Weobley 14 A3
Werrington 3 C11
West Bergholt. . . . 25 N4
Westbourne. 9 G12
West Bridgford . . . 22 B4
West Bromwich . . . 21 G11
West Burton 32 F2
Westbury
  Shrops 20 F4
  Wilts. 8 C3
Westbury-on-
  Severn 14 E6
Westbury-sub-
  Mendip. 7 G14
West Calder. 40 G3
West Coker 5 B9
Westcott. 10 E2
West Dean 8 E7
West End 9 K10
Westerham 10 D5
West Felton. 20 D4
Westfield 11 H9
West Grinstead. . . . 10 G2
West Haddon 22 H5
Westhill 50 G7
Westhoughton . . . 26 E7
West Kilbride . . . 38 F7

West Kingsdown 10 C6
West Kirby 26 G3
Westleton. 25 J9
West Linton 40 H4
West Looe 3 F10
West Lulworth. 8 K3
West Malling 10 D7
West Meon. 9 E11
West Mersea. 25 P5
Westminster. 10 A4
West Moors. 8 G5
Weston. 21 D10
Weston-super-Mare. 7 E12
Westonzoyland. 7 H12
West Rasen 29 F9
Westruther. 41 H9
West Thorney 9 G12
Westward Ho!. 6 J3
West Wellow 9 F8
West Woodburn . . . 36 E7
Wetheral. 36 H3
Wetherby. 32 K6
Wetwang 33 J11
Weybourne. 24 A6
Weybridge. 16 J5
Weyhill. 9 C8
Weymouth 5 F10
Whaley Bridge . . . 27 G11
Whalley. 27 B8
Whalton. 37 E10
Whatton. 22 B6
Whauphill. 34 J5
Whaw. 32 D1
Wheathampstead. . . 16 D6
Wheatley
  Notts 28 F6
  Oxon. 15 F14
Wheatley Hill. 37 K12
Wheaton Aston. . . . 21 E9
Wheldrake 33 K8
Whicham 30 F7
Whickham 37 G11
Whimple. 4 D4
Whipsnade. 16 D5
Whissendine 22 D7
Whitburn 40 G2
Whitby. 33 C10
Whitchurch
  Bristol 14 K5
  Bucks. 16 D3
  Devon. 3 D12
  Hants 9 C9
  Hereford 14 E4
  Shrops 20 B6
White Bridge. 48 G5
Whitehall Village. . . 56 D6
Whitehaven. 30 C5
Whitehouse. 38 D3
Whitekirk. 41 E9
Whiteparish. 8 E7
Whitfield 11 E14
Whithorn 34 K5
Whitland. 12 E5
Whitley Bay 37 F12
Whitonditch 15 J11
Whitsome. 41 H11
Whitstable. 11 C12
Whitstone 3 B10
Whittington
  Derbys 28 G2
  Lancs. 31 G12
  Shrops 20 C4
  Staffs 21 F12
Whittlebury 16 A1
Whittlesey 23 F11
Whittlesford 17 A9
Whitwell
  Derbys 28 G4
  IoW 9 K10
Whitwick. 22 D3
Whitworth 27 D9
Whixley. 32 J6
Whome. 56 G3
Wick
  Hants 8 F6
  Highland. 53 D15
  V Glam 13 J13

Wicken 23 H14
Wickford. 17 F12
Wickham 9 G10
Wickham Market . . . 25 K8
Wickwar. 14 H6
Widdrington 37 D11
Widecombe in the
  Moor. 4 F1
Widemouth Bay 3 A9
Wide Open. 37 F11
Widnes. 26 G6
Wigan. 26 E6
Wigmore
  Hereford 20 K5
  Medway 11 C9
Wigston. 22 F5
Wigton. 35 J13
Wigtown. 34 H5
Wilkhaven. 53 K11
Willand 4 C4
Willaston. 26 H4
Willenhall. 21 F10
Willersley. 14 B2
Willesborough 11 E11
Willingdon. 10 J7
Willington
  Bedford 16 A6
  Durham 37 K10
Williton. 7 H9
Willoughby 29 G13
Wilmington 4 D6
Wilmslow. 27 G9
Wilnecote. 21 F13
Wilton. 8 D6
Wimblington. 23 F13
Wimborne Minster . 8 H5
Wincanton. 5 A11
Winchcombe. 15 D9
Winchelsea 11 H10
Winchester 9 E9
Windermere 31 E10
Windsor. 16 H4
Windygates 40 C6
Wing. 16 C3
Wingate. 37 K13
Wingham. 11 D13
Winkleigh. 3 A14
Winscombe. 7 F13
Winsford. 26 J7
Winslow. 16 C2
Winster. 27 J13
Winston. 32 C3
Winterborne
  Stickland. 8 G3
Winterbourne Abbas. 5 E10
Winterton
  N Lincs. 29 C8
  Norf 24 C9
Wirksworth 28 J1
Wisbech. 23 D13
Wisbech St Mary . 23 E13
Wisborough Green . 10 G1
Wishaw. 39 E13
Witchampton 8 G4
Witchford. 23 H14
Witham. 17 D13
Witheridge. 4 A15
Withern. 29 F13
Withernsea. 29 B12
Withington. 15 E9
Witley. 9 D14
Witnesham 25 K6
Witney. 15 E12
Wittersham 11 G10
Wiveliscombe 7 J9
Wivelsfield. 10 G4
Wivenhoe. 25 N5
Wix. 25 N6
Woburn. 16 B4
Woburn Sands . . . 16 B4
Woking. 16 K5
Wokingham. 16 J3
Wolf's Castle. . . . 12 D3
Wollaston. 23 J8
Wolsingham 37 K9
Wolverhampton . . . 21 G10
Wolverton 16 B3

Wolviston. 32 B6
Wombwell 28 D2
Wonersh. 10 E1
Wonston. 9 D9
Woodbridge 25 L7
Woodbury 4 E4
Woodchester. 14 F7
Woodchurch 11 F10
Woodcote 16 G1
Woodgreen 8 F6
Woodhall Spa 29 H11
Woodhouse. 28 F3
Woodhouse Eaves . . 22 D4
Woodley. 16 H2
Woodstock. 15 E13
Woofferton 20 K6
Wookey. 7 G14
Wookey Hole 7 G14
Wool. 8 J3
Woolacombe. 6 G3
Woolavington . . . 7 G12
Wooler. 37 A8
Woolwich. 10 B5
Woolwich Ferry . . . 10 B5
Wooperton. 37 A9
Woore. 21 B8
Wootton Bridge . . . 9 H10
Wootton Wawen. . . 21 K12
Worcester 14 A7
Worfield 21 G8
Workington 30 B5
Worksop. 28 G4
Wormit. 40 A6
Worsbrough. 28 D2
Wortham 24 H5
Worthing 10 J2
Wotton under Edge . 14 G6
Wragby. 29 G12
Wrangle 29 J13
Wrea Green 26 B4
Wrentham. 24 G9
Wretham 24 G4
Wrexham. 20 A4
Writtle. 17 E11
Wroughton 15 J10
Wroxham 24 D7
Wroxton 15 B13
Wyberton 23 A11
Wye. 11 E11
Wylye. 8 D5
Wymondham
  Leics. 22 D7
  Norf 24 E6

Y

Yalding. 11 E8
Yarcombe. 4 C6
Yardley Hastings. . . 22 K7
Yarm. 32 C6
Yarmouth 9 J8
Yarnton. 15 E13
Yarrow. 36 A2
Yate. 14 H6
Yatton. 7 E13
Yaxley. 23 F10
Yeadon. 27 A12
Yealmpton 3 F13
Yelverton 3 E13
Yeovil. 5 B9
Yetminster 5 C9
Y Felinheli 18 D5
York. 32 J7
Youlgreave. 27 J13
Yoxall. 21 E12
Yoxford. 25 J8
Ysbyty Ifan . . . 18 F8
Ysbyty Ystwyth . . . 19 N7
Ystalyfera. 13 F11
Ystradgynlais . . . 13 E11

Z

Zennor 2 H2